The Manager's Guide to Mediating Conflict

Learn how to confidently mediate conflicts in the workplace

Alison Love

Impackt Publishing
We Mean Business

The Manager's Guide to Mediating Conflict

Copyright © 2014 Impackt Publishing

First published: September 2014

Production reference: 1240914

Published by Impackt Publishing Ltd.
Livery Place
35 Livery Street
Birmingham B3 2PB, UK.

ISBN 978-1-78300-066-1

www.Impacktpub.com

Credits

Author
Alison Love

Reviewers
Arslan Ali
Roy Cheng

Commissioning Editor
Richard Gall

Copy Editors
Simran Bhogal
Ameesha Green
Faisal Siddiqui

Project Coordinator
Venitha Cutinho

Proofreader
Maria Gould

Production Coordinator
Melwyn D'sa

Cover Work
Simon Cardew

About the Author

Alison Love has over 30 years of practical experience as an HR practitioner, employment lawyer, and a business leader. Prior to qualifying as a solicitor, she spent 8 years as an HR practitioner in the public, retail, and consumer finance sectors. This, combined with her skills and experience as a workplace mediator, has given Alison a unique understanding of the dynamics of workplace issues and an ability to successfully facilitate parties in identifying solutions. Having witnessed the limitations of the legal process and the benefits and power of mediation, Alison has firsthand experience of demonstrating that workplace mediation provides a better way to resolve conflict in the workplace in the vast majority of cases. Alison is passionate about sharing her knowledge and making mediation the first choice in resolving workplace disputes.

Alison currently runs her own business (Alison Love Limited) which provides workplace mediation and dispute resolution services, including mediation, associated training, and executive coaching.

Alison lives in Wales with her husband, two sons, and Jaffa the dog, where she can often be found walking Jaffa or pursuing her interest in photography. Alison also enjoys travelling, live music, and the occasional mad cycling challenge.

My thanks go to the team at Impackt who have guided me through the process of writing this guide. Thanks also go to my family; to my husband, Steve, who has (as usual) shown a great deal of patience and support and my sons, Daniel and Alex, for providing cooked meals for themselves and for me (from time to time).

About the Reviewers

Arslan Ali has more than 14 years of experience related to the IT industry and training institutions with exclusive experience of 5 years in teaching various disciplines and projects in an IT institution. He has worked in various roles in software engineering, software testing, training, and quality assurance. The major focus of his expertise lies in coordination, implementation, and testing of ERPs and customized applications. He is also a trainer for context-driven testing for various companies and individuals.

Arslan is currently working at Sidat Hyder Morshed Associates as a senior consultant in Information Solutions, but besides that he is also an active founding member of TestersTestified (www.testerstestified.com) (@testtified), Outtabox! (www.outtabox.co) (@OuttaBoxPk), and OISOL – Open Integrated Solutions (www.oisol.com) as a training consultant for software testing and context-driven testing workshops.

You can follow him on Twitter, @arslan0644, and on LinkedIn at pk.linkedin.com/in/thegoodchanges/.

I would like to thank Impackt publishing for this opportunity and my father for his reading habits which he successfully passed on to me!

Roy Cheng is an Adjunct Lecturer (The University of Hong Kong, School of Professional And Continuing Education (HKU SPACE)), Founder and Director of Hong Kong Institute of Mediation Limited, Director of ISE Consultants Limited, and a certified trainer of the Mediation Training Institute of the U.S.A. (MTI). He is currently a mediation practitioner, mediator accreditation assessor, and a mediation program trainer. Prior to commencing his dispute resolution practice, he had extensive commercial experiences in a wide range of industries. In 2004, he was invited by the Hong Kong Home Affairs Department and successfully mediated the Albert House Case and in 2006, he was invited by Hong Kong Housing Authority and successfully mediated the Dickson Construction subcontractor disputes. He has also written a book a book in Chinese about interest-based negotiation approach which is commonly used in mediation: "調解：談判突破困局" (the English title is "Getting to Harmony"). First published in March 2009, the book is now in its fifth edition.

Contents

> Preface

With over 30 years of experience as an HR practitioner and employment lawyer, I have witnessed and advised on more workplace disputes than I care to remember. I began to see the same patterns recurring and the outcomes being less than positive for the organizations or the individuals concerned. Disputes would generally involve considerable expense and management time and often end in a painful exit of an employee who was once highly regarded.

I began to think that there must be a better way; to me, traditional grievances or disciplinary processes were causing considerable harm to individuals and businesses, and the current mechanisms used to resolve disputes were not fit for purpose. These processes were becoming more and more legalistic and adversarial, concerned with imposing a decision by a third-party rather than bringing those concerned together and resolving matters directly between them. When I started to look into mediation, I began to understand how mediation offers something very different from the more traditional processes; I had what I would describe as a "light bulb" moment. I soon realized that mediation is an empowering alternative that in the vast majority of cases will provide far better outcomes with considerable cost savings. I now look back at some particularly painful cases that I was involved in litigating; if mediation had been an option then, I am convinced that it would all have been far less painful and less costly. I also realized that the skills that you learn to become an effective mediator are key people management skills that enhance employee relations, enabling teams to use conflict positively and improve performance.

It is clear that workplace conflict and the costs associated with it are on the rise. If these costs could be reduced, there would undoubtedly be a positive impact on the bottom line. It is estimated that a staggering 25 percent of managers' time is spent in dealing with workplace conflict. If conflict remains unresolved or a formal process is followed, the divide between the individuals widens, communication becomes guarded or ceases altogether, and the conflict deepens and becomes more entrenched. The inevitable results are damage to an individual's wellbeing, increased sickness absence, and reduced levels of engagement, motivation, and productivity, as well as a possible loss of talent. The Advisory, Conciliation, and Arbitration Service (ACAS) suggests that the cost of mediation is half that of pursuing a formal process, while others suggest it is a fifth; either way it is a considerable saving. If litigation or settlements follow, these are additional, and often substantial costs are incurred on top of the indirect costs. In contrast, mediation will usually conclude in one day with most providers reporting success rates of 90 percent. While there is some debate about what success means, there is no doubt that the business case for mediation is very strong.

I am now a passionate convert to workplace and employment mediation. It should and could be used in far more cases than it currently is. This book is designed to share my revelations and to encourage you to have the confidence to use meditation skills and processes to the benefit of employees and organizations alike.

Mediation skills can also be used to help positively manage conflict on a day-to-day basis so that conflict becomes constructive rather than destructive. This in itself produces huge benefits. I do not exaggerate when I say that every conflict situation that I have come across could and should have been resolved much earlier with the right management intervention. Far too often, situations are left to fester until there is a tipping point. By this time, much damage has already been done and the conflict is harder to resolve.

My hope is that this book will also help to equip you with the skills to prevent situations escalating to this point and to help you resolve those situations that have. If I achieve any of that, even in part, I will be happy! Not only will I have made individuals' lives and relationships better, I will also have saved organizations a considerable cost. **Happy days!**

What this book covers

Chapter 1, Conflict in the Workplace, looks closely at some of the key principles behind the contemporary understanding of conflict and how it arises in the context of the workplace.

Chapter 2, Mediator Skill Set, gives you the skills and strategies you need for an effective and successful mediation process.

Chapter 3, The Mediation Process, will take you through the typical framework of mediation, including the necessary legal information, as well as some advice on how to get the most effective results.

Chapter 4, Beyond the Mediation, gives you guidance and information about what needs to be done after the process to ensure that positive results are maintained and that the parties involved are both satisfied.

Who this book is for

If you are in any kind of leadership position at work and want to find a more effective method of dealing with conflict at work, this book is for you. Whether people management is one of your core responsibilities or something that you value as an important part of business leadership, I will help you get a strong understanding of what mediation is and, more importantly, how to do it quickly and effectively to build a stronger team and minimize negative conflicts. Once you have a strong grasp on the principles of negotiation, the core skills and ideas you will learn in this book will strengthen your leadership skills more generally.

Conventions

In this book, you will find a number of styles of text that distinguish between different kinds of information. Here are some examples of these styles, and an explanation of their meaning.

New terms and **important words** are shown in bold.

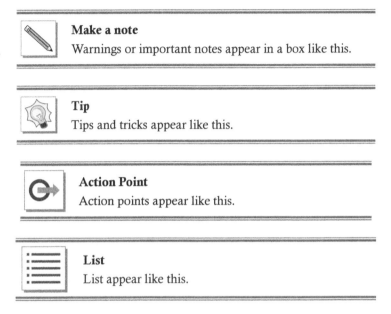

> **Make a note**
> Warnings or important notes appear in a box like this.

> **Tip**
> Tips and tricks appear like this.

> **Action Point**
> Action points appear like this.

> **List**
> List appear like this.

Reader feedback

Feedback from our readers is always welcome. Let us know what you think about this book—what you liked or may have disliked. Reader feedback is important for us to develop titles that you really get the most out of.

To send us general feedback, simply send an e-mail to feedback@impacktpub.com, and mention the book title via the subject of your message.

If there is a book that you need and would like to see us publish, please send us a note via the **Submit Idea** form on https://www.impacktpub.com/#!/bookidea.

Piracy

Piracy of copyright material on the Internet is an ongoing problem across all media. At Packt, we take the protection of our copyright and licenses very seriously. If you come across any illegal copies of our works, in any form, on the Internet, please provide us with the location address or website name immediately so that we can pursue a remedy.

Please contact us at `copyright@impacktpub.com` with a link to the suspected pirated material.

We appreciate your help in protecting our authors, and our ability to bring you valuable content.

1

Conflict in the Workplace

"The opposite of a profound truth may well be another profound truth"

—Niels Bohr, Danish physicist

An understanding of the key principles of conflict and the impact it has on individuals will help you to understand why mediation can be so effective. Understanding the foundational ideas upon which the concept of mediation is built will give you a greater sense of the skills needed to mediate and facilitate workplace disputes. By acknowledging some of the causes of conflict in a contemporary office environment, you will gain a stronger understanding of exactly when and how you should take action.

Redefining conflict

At its core, conflict is very simply a different point of view; the differences being due to our varied experiences, views of the world, and cultures or values. All of these elements give us different perspectives and influence how we see things.

Conflict is not about who is right or who is wrong. It is about the different way that we see and interpret things. Individuals often get stuck in conflict situations because they get caught up in questions around truth, intentions, and blame. In terms of resolving conflict, then, who is right and wrong isn't important; what is fundamental is understanding and accepting differing perspectives. Your role as a mediator is to facilitate the parties in achieving this; it is about helping the parties to better understand each other sufficiently rather than getting the parties to agree with each other.

In the vast majority of the mediations that I have been involved in, the specific facts and issues of a dispute often fall away very quickly and become irrelevant. What's left are differing perspectives and hurt feelings fuelled by misunderstanding, miscommunication, distrust, and speculation over the intentions of others. As a mediator, you need to tackle all of these things and not be afraid to do so. Resolution can only come from the emotional aspects of disputes being aired and understood.

Helping parties to shift their focus away from establishing who is right and who is wrong towards acknowledging the impact of the conflict on each other and understanding each other's perspective is a key principle in resolving conflict. This can range from giving the individuals themselves the support and skills to resolve conflict positively to interventions from others, including informal action by you as the line manager or by adopting the role of a mediator.

The rise in workplace disputes

If you find yourself spending increasing amounts of time dealing with workplace conflicts, managing the impact on an individual's performance, and being dragged into formal processes that are rarely helpful, then you are not alone! Numerous surveys report that there has been a considerable increase in workplace conflict in recent years and the time taken to resolve these conflicts using formal processes (disciplinary and grievance processes) has also increased. In addition, employment tribunal claims continue to rise year on year. The rise in conflict does vary from sector to sector with the public sector in the UK experiencing considerably higher numbers of disputes than in the private sector. One study suggests that the IT and Construction sectors have the lowest levels and organizational culture, management accountability, and conflict management skills all have an impact. Over 40 percent of conflicts are said to relate to relationship issues and this is consistent across all sectors (CIPD Employee Relations Survey 2011 and Workplace (UK) Conflict Survey 2011). While the context and extent of conflict can vary, it can arise anywhere and the skills and processes to positively resolve conflict, which we will discuss in later chapters, are in themselves important in promoting a culture that reduces the levels of destructive conflict and costly disputes.

So why is there so much conflict in the modern workplace? The reasons are incredibly diverse, but all circulate around the central issue of different perspectives, as the following figure illustrates. Some of these problems are explored in more detail in the following list.

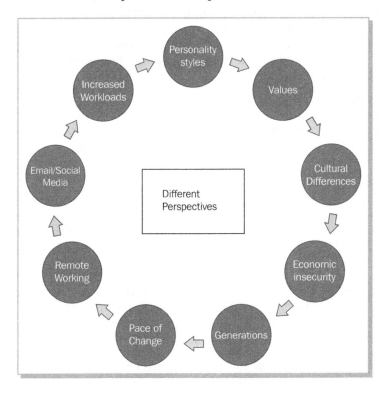

> **Increasing workloads**: This is now considered to be the primary cause of conflict. In the current economic climate, the result of staff cuts or funding cuts often lead to employees being asked to do more work with less resources. Problems also arise in relation to the fair allocation of work between individuals or where employees are being asked to take on new and different tasks.

> **Personality conflicts**: These are very common in practice and are reported to be the second most common cause of conflict. We all have different personality traits that impact on our preferred working and communication styles and ability (or otherwise) to manage relationships. Certain styles are more likely to clash with each other than others. Problems arise if these differences are not understood, accepted, or managed.

> **Globalization**: This results in more employees from different cultures working together than ever before.

> **Lack of job opportunities**: Employees cannot leave and find alternative jobs and so are forced to remain in conflict situations when previously they would have "walked".

> **Job insecurity and economic worries**: These impact individuals' stress levels, which reduce the ability to manage relationships and conflicts positively.

> ➤ **Inter-generational differences**: With the abolition of retirement ages and huge variations in the demographics of the workforce, differing work ethics, communication styles, and values are starting to impact. Generation X and Y tend not to respond positively to the more traditional management practices, engage and use technology in different ways, and their expectations of work tend to vary from those of the older generations. In some cases, disputes may arise as a result of older workers extending their working lives and blocking opportunities for younger workers.

> ➤ **Pace of change**: Organizational changes created by the constant need to innovate can also create conflict as change can be difficult and stressful for many employees to cope with or adapt to. If not implemented properly, change can create fear, resentment, and questions of unfair treatment.

> ➤ **New ways of working and communicating**: In particular new modes of communication and remote working can significantly reduce the opportunities for face-to-face communication. This increases the chances of communication being misunderstood and less effective. E-mail communications or the use of social media, for example, often cause problems as much of the communication (contained in such things as body language, tone of voice, and facial expressions) is missing.

While you may have little influence over many of these issues, you can still do a lot to prevent these causes damaging working relationships and creating ongoing conflict. The details on how conflict can be prevented in these situations is beyond the remit of this book, but some useful tips to bear in mind are as follows:

1. **Don't avoid the problem**: In all the cases that I have been involved in, the situation could either have been avoided all together or improved if some action had been taken at an earlier stage. In practice, the vast majority of conflicts become destructive and damaging because a "difficult conversation" is avoided rather than tackled, or a manager has failed to intervene. Avoidance is never a good policy as resentments fester and communication suffers; what was a small issue to start with becomes something far more significant. So my advice is to always tackle the problem rather than avoid it and intervene early.

2. **Skill up**: By utilizing the mediation and conflict management resolution skills in the next chapter, you can tackle these issues in a positive and constructive way.

3. **Engage and communicate**: An increased level of engagement and communication with employees is important in helping you avoid and manage disputes. Whenever possible, you should invest the time in face-to-face communication and really listen to them. If you know your employees and understand what is important to them and their values and motivations, then you can adapt your management style and anticipate problems. If you build up an open and trusting relationship and know your employees you are more likely to spot problems arising and it is easier to have the difficult conversations and get to the root of any problems.

4. **Watch out for stress**: There is a clear link between stress and conflict. A common example is when conflict arises from increased workloads or the enforced rapid adaptation to organizational change. Stress also leads to a decline in an individual's ability to deal with conflict situations appropriately so the situation spirals and worsens. Therefore, you should do what you can to reduce stress as far as possible. This can be achieved by things such as providing employees with as much control as possible over their workload, increased involvement in decision making, improved engagement and communication, and flexibility in how and when employees work.

5. **Pay attention in times of change**: When change is being implemented, the need to engage and communicate is even greater. It will help if employees understand the reasons for the change and are clear on how the change process will be managed. Communication should be constant throughout the process so that employees are kept up to date. If employees are struggling with the changes, do not ignore this; communicate and listen some more and demonstrate patience and empathy.

Prevention, as they say, is always better than cure, so these steps are essential to prevent conflict escalating and to tackle any issues that may require mediation later down the road. The techniques and skills used in mediation, however, are useful in more informal settings, so don't think that mediation is only an option once an issue or situation has escalated.

Good versus bad conflict

Bringing different perspectives and different points of view together should be a positive thing, and it should help promote creativity and innovation. So while we tend to think of conflict in negative terms, it can be a force for good. If conflict is managed positively or the culture is such that it promotes a healthy exchange of viewpoints, this promotes understanding and allows individuals to express opinions in a constructive way that achieves collaboration and engagement; all of which is positive. Patrick Lencioni, in his book *The Five Dysfunctions of a Team*, lists the fear of conflict as one of the five dysfunctions of a team and that teams who develop the ability to engage in healthy conflict and open debate will move towards high performance. Indeed it could be argued that a fear of conflict and reluctance to challenge may well have contributed to some of the dramatic corporate scandals of recent history, such as Enron, Goldman Sachs, and HBOS.

Lencioni suggests that teams that fear conflict will tend to have boring meetings, engage in personal attacks and power politics, ignore controversial topics, fail to tap into all opinions, and waste time and energy with posturing and interpersonal risk management. I am sure we can all relate to this and have witnessed this to varying degrees. A team that engages in conflict positively will in contrast have lively and interesting meetings, exploit ideas from all, solve problems quickly, minimize politics, and put critical topics on the table for discussion (rather than avoid them).

A manager's style of leadership will have a big influence on whether a team can engage in healthy conflict. If a manager leads by example, they themselves encourage open debate and manage conflict in a positive way; this will influence others to do likewise. Also, in a team or culture where there is healthy conflict, the individuals will be empowered to take responsibility to resolve issues between themselves. Lencioni suggests that team members should have the confidence to identify buried disagreements and encourage the team to resolve them. Understanding others' typical responses to conflict can also help here. Ideally the manager should not be called on or be required to intervene in every issue; if the parties can resolve matters themselves then they should be given the opportunity to do so. It is only where this is not possible or successful that the manager will need to take action. The trick is of course to identify when this is necessary. To put yourself into a position where you can spot when this is required, it is necessary to take the time and effort to really know and understand those who work with you and be alert to differences in behaviors, communications, relationships, and engagement.

Problems arise when the culture does not encourage healthy conflict, conflict is not managed positively, or it remains unresolved for long periods of time. In these situations conflict becomes damaging; in turn, this creates a relational crisis that destabilizes people. As a result, people act and react in ways that produce unproductive and destructive dynamics.

Unfortunately, conflict remains unresolved or is simply avoided in far too many situations; it is estimated that 60 percent of line managers tend to avoid conflict rather than seek to tackle and resolve it (CIPD Leadership and Management of Conflict Survey 2008). As we all know from our own personal experiences, ignoring or avoiding conflict does not produce a positive result; rather, it worsens the situation. Resentments fester, communication diminishes, and individuals begin to get stuck in the conflict situation so that the need for some third-party intervention (such as mediation) increases.

Conflict, then, can be both productive and harmful. Some of the ways in which conflict can have a positive effect are as follows:

> **Innovation**: A workplace where people are able to discuss, argue, and take different positions is essential if you are looking to cultivate a work environment where new ideas are encouraged and even required.

> **Creativity**: Similarly, creativity is something that is developed through interaction and, indeed, friendly conflict with others. To think creatively, you sometimes need a sounding board, even if it is a dissenting voice!

> **Engagement**: Conflict, in its proper place, actually correlates with the engagement of employees. Indeed, good conflict is a symptom rather than a cause of engagement, but it indicates that employees feel empowered and committed enough to their roles to feel passionately about and stimulated by their tasks.

> **Personal development**: Good conflict is also an essential part of one's personal development. While the phrase "what doesn't kill you makes you stronger" may or may not be true, in this case, good conflict is intrinsic to personal development in the sense that it is indicative of the fact that you are offering a fresh perspective, that you are actively contributing to something, or having an effect on the way things are done.

Of course, there is always another side to this, and often it is the inverse that leads to bad conflict. So, bad conflict could be the result of a lack of innovation in a workplace. If there is no sense of progression, or a desire to improve, this will lead to frustration and even stress, which, in turn, leads to bad conflict. One might consider conflict as being buried within any situation; think for example, of a good friendship—the best friendships often feature some kind of antagonism or conflict which make them interesting and stimulating. The problem happens when this conflict or what might be called productive antagonism becomes stifled. It's then redirected, producing frustration, irritation, and as I will now explore, stress.

The impact of stress

As indicated in the preceding section, stress caused by such things as organizational change or increasing workloads can in itself contribute to conflict arising. In addition, where individuals are in conflict, one or usually both parties will almost always be in a state of stress so the situation will worsen. Understanding how stress impacts individuals and how this impacts the ability to deal with conflict situations is important to understand. I now look back on disputes that I was involved in litigating and appreciate why parties acted in the way that they did. Had I understood this at the time, I am sure that this would have helped me advise people better and influence the way that matters were handled.

Essentially, stress makes us stupid. The neurological impact of stress is that blood in our brains moves from the frontal area which is the logical thinking part of our brains to the subcortical area, which is the emotional part where the flight or fight response modes are activated.

This means that the logical thinking parts of our brain are blocked by the instinctive flight or fight response modes. The following are some of the consequences of this:

> ➤ Our ability to focus is weakened

> ➤ Our minds keep being dragged back to the object of tension (such as the conflict)

> ➤ We do not listen properly and communication suffers

> ➤ We react in inappropriate ways, for example by responding aggressively or withdrawing

> ➤ We see ill motive and a conspiracy theory in everything that is said or done

> ➤ We jump to conclusions too quickly and respond too violently to events that in the bigger scheme of things seem totally unimportant

> ➤ We are not able to relate to others as effectively

It is important to appreciate that individuals will be reacting in these ways throughout a mediation process. In order to help them return to a position where they can listen and respond appropriately, it is first necessary to help individuals to get out of their state of stress. There are very simple exercises that you can encourage others to do to relieve stress. For example, concentrating on breathing deeply is highly effective; an excellent way to do this is to practice 7/11 breathing. This is where you breathe in for seven and breathe out for eleven. It is the ratio that is important so that you are breathing in for less time that you breathe out. Another technique is to improve your posture by imagining a balloon on a string from the top of your head. It may sound a bit odd but these two very simple exercises are highly effective. If in doubt, try it next time you feel stressed; I guarantee you will start to feel calmer.

Also as a mediator, you can help reduce stress by acknowledging the emotions of the parties, being empathetic and understanding, demonstrating real deep listening, giving individuals sufficient time, having patience, and establishing and maintaining calmness throughout. Remember that your mood as the mediator will affect the parties.

Whether you are in an active mediation process or simply managing the stresses and strains of your employees, dealing with stress effectively is essential, and the skills that you will use in a mediation scenario can be used every day to help your employees and colleagues.

How mediation differs from other conflict resolutions

Where there is a workplace dispute, there are a number of options that can be used to deal with it. These range from allowing parties to resolve it themselves through to litigation, as set out in the conflict resolution road map.

The differences between mediation and other options are shown in the following image:

	Resolution by parties/manages	Mediation	Grievance/Disciplinary	Legal Proceedings
Parties have power to resolve?	✔	✔	✘	✘
Decision imposed by third party?	✘	✘	✔	✔
Emotional aspect considered?	✔	✔	✘	✘
Process confidential?	✔	✔	✘	✘
Process Without Prejudice	✘	✔	✘	✘
Rights taken into account?	✘	✘	✔	✔
Factual dispute resolved?	✘	✘	✔	✔

With all options other than mediation, the focus will be on the party's rights and the outcome will depend on a decision from a third-party as to whose rights are preferred; the emotional aspect is completely ignored as it is irrelevant to the process. Particularly where there is an ongoing relationship, this will rarely result in a positive outcome. Individuals will become defensive, communication will either cease all together or be very guarded and the gap between them will widen. I have seen many grievance processes resulting in further damaging relations, making an already bad situation a million times worse.

Mediation, unlike other formal processes or litigation, addresses the underlying emotions and in practice it is important to do so and to avoid shying away from this. In mediation who is right and who is wrong is entirely irrelevant and it puts the power to resolve matters in the hands of the parties. In this way, mediation is far more likely to produce a positive result, either allowing employees to work together in a better way or enabling an exit on better terms. As Kenneth Cloke puts it brilliantly in his book *Mediating Dangerously*, "the purpose of the search for truth in conflict resolution is twofold; first, to help the parties achieve a substantially fair result; and second, to help them feel a result is fair, allowing the wounds to heal."

Deciding to use mediation

Although mediation is a far better option, in the vast majority of cases it will not always be appropriate. The following table illustrates when to consider using mediation and when it will not be appropriate.

In terms of timing, I would urge you to always consider using mediation at the earliest possible stage. If you believe a situation is likely to result in some kind of formal process then mediation should begin prior to that process. Not only does this increase the chances of the mediation being successful, it also reduces the time and cost expended. Many of the mediations I have conducted have followed a lengthy and painful formal process, which has exacerbated the situation and could have been avoided in its entirety.

Consider mediation	Mediation not appropriate
Prior to a formal disciplinary/grievance For example: ■ Where performance issues are linked to allegations of poor management or supervision or difficulties with colleagues ■ Where employees are showing signs of stress due to relationship difficulties with others ■ Informal grievances or complaints related to poor working relationships or management style	No agreement of the parties (Conflict coaching or other support to help employees manage and resolve the conflict can be an alternative here.)
Unresolved/inconclusive grievances For example: ■ The grievance has done nothing to improve working relations or has made matters worse ■ No findings have been possible due to conflicts of evidence and unsubstantiated allegations ■ One party has been absent for a period of time and is now returning to work following a grievance or disciplinary	Some gross misconduct offences For example: ■ Those involving dishonesty or serious offences which may also amount to a criminal offence or where there are serious health and safety

Consider mediation	Mediation not appropriate
Implementation of major changes/re-organizations For example: ■ Where employees consider that changes are being implemented unfairly on them ■ Employees are struggling to cope with changes and are resistant	Where there is a need for a message, for example, serious discrimination/harassment For example: ■ Where the employer wants to send a message to the workforce generally that certain misconduct will not be tolerated
Collective/industrial relations disputes For example: ■ Where other dispute resolution mechanisms have failed to resolve disputes with trade unions ■ Where a team has become dysfunctional due to the breakdown of relationships between team members	Where the mental health of a party is a concern For example: ■ Where there is doubt regarding an individual's ability to properly participate and make rational decisions
On-going difficulties in working relationships For example: ■ Where employees need to co-operate and work together but are struggling to do so and there is an impact on them and/or those around them ■ Where there has been a breakdown of trust and confidence	
Boardroom disputes For example: ■ Where senior executives are in conflict, unable to communicate effectively and there is an impact on the collective decision making at senior level	

Ideally I would suggest that mediation be considered as a first option in the vast majority of cases, with formal procedures being the exception to the rule. In order to encourage parties to enter into mediation in preference to formal processes, you may need to work at explaining what mediation is and highlight the benefits. It is also helpful to have mediation written into policies as a first step. You might think that as a mediator I would say that, wouldn't you!

Conflict road map

Mediation is part of a bigger picture of conflict resolution. It is always useful to have this in mind to gain some sense of perspective and context as to how mediation fits into the larger process of resolving conflict, as this will enable you to gain a greater handle on the conflict and where you are trying to get to with the mediation. The following figure represents a road map of conflict resolution. This should enable you to successfully manage any conflict situation in a way that is appropriate and effective.

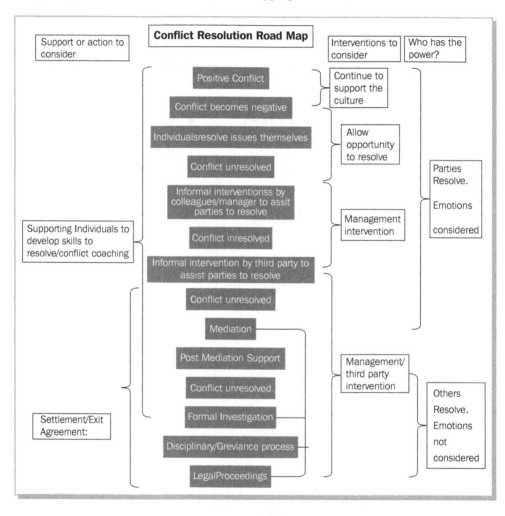

Summary

You should now have a better understanding of how and why a conflict arises in workplace situations and also the impact that this has on individuals and relationships. This should give you an appreciation of why mediation can be so effective in resolving conflicts. This in itself gives you a head start in becoming an effective mediator. Finally, you should now be able to identify and spot those situations where conflict may arise and when to take action.

The next chapter builds on this by looking at the specific skills required to be an effective mediator.

>2

Mediator Skill Set

The key skills that a mediator needs will be outlined in this chapter together with some tips on how to put these into practice and how they relate to the mediation process. As with any skills, they will improve over time and with practice and experience. The following are the key skills required, which we will explore in more detail throughout this chapter. Used together, these skills will enable you to manage the process confidently and effectively while maintaining control and establishing authority.

- ➤ **Deep listening skills**: This is probably the single most important (and possibly most difficult) skill to master. This also involves being empathetic but not being drawn in

- ➤ **Establish trust and rapport**: As a mediator, you need to be able to quickly gain the trust of the parties and establish and build rapport

- ➤ **An ability to retain a sense of calmness**: If you remain cool, calm, and collected, and manage your own emotions, then those around you will be influenced by this

- ➤ **Neutrality and independence**: It is vital that both parties feel that they are being treated equally

- ➤ **Creativity**: The ability to offer innovative solutions and to identify needs and interests and common threads is paramount in mediation

- ➤ **Questioning skills**: Good questioning techniques and reframing statements encourage parties to look at things differently and seek solutions

- ➤ **Confidentiality**: You must honor the confidentiality of the process; otherwise, trust and confidence will be lost and your credibility will be completely undermined

Let's look at these in some more detail—if you can master these, you will be well on your way to becoming an effective mediator.

Deep listening skills

To listen fully means to pay attention to what is being said beneath the words. You listen not only to the "music", but to the essence of the person speaking. You listen not only for what a person knows, but for what he or she is.

–Peter Senge

Listening skills are the single most important skill that a mediator needs to master. Most of us are not good at listening; we are taught to speak, to write, and to read, but we are not taught to listen. With practice, however, you can improve your listening skills.

As a mediator, you need to learn to listen at a deep emphatic level, which requires real and sustained concentration. Empathetic listening means that you listen to more than the words that are spoken. You need to listen to the emotions and feelings underneath the words and to the non-verbal communication. It is also important that you demonstrate to the other person that you have listened and understood. However hard you might try, it is impossible to multitask while listening (I have tried and failed many times!).

The following are some useful tips to achieve real deep emphatic listening.

Prepare yourself

You have to be in the right frame of mind yourself. Relax your posture and suspend your concerns and thoughts. If you go into a mediation thinking about all the other things on your "to-do list", what you are having for dinner, or who is picking up your kids, you will not give the other person (or people) your full attention. People have different techniques to achieve this but the breathing and posture exercises referred to in *Chapter 1, Conflict in the Workplace*, to relieve stress also work well here. A good way to leave your personal issues behind is to write them on a piece of paper and then file it away, usually in a bin.

Listen for the emotion

Try to identify the speaker's feelings and emotions by listening to what is beneath the words. Pay attention to tone of voice and body language as well as what is not said. Silence can speak volumes! Where the words that are spoken are at variance with the body language and tone, the vast majority of the message communicated comes from non-verbal signals, so pay particular attention if this is the case.

Be empathetic

Empathy means that you step into the thoughts and feelings of the speaker and understand them. This is distinguished from sympathy, which is where you feel the same emotions as the other person. Sympathy should be avoided as you need to adopt a more detached approach. The problem or issue is not yours and it is not wise to take it on your own shoulders. Not only is this not healthy for you, it will almost certainly impact on your ability to remain neutral. Similarly you need to avoid antipathy, that is, having a deep dislike of a particular view point. A good example would be where you come across something that is deeply offensive to your own personal values, such as discrimination or bullying. I find that a good way to remain sufficiently detached is to think of yourself looking down on the parties from a balcony. Also when listening to one party, always bear in mind that what you will hear from the other will be an entirely different story, so suspend any judgment.

Check your understanding and demonstrate you are listening

Check to make sure you have understood the speaker and heard the details correctly. This is equally important for the purposes of ensuring that the parties feel really listened to and understood. This can be achieved in a number of ways, including the following:

> Summarizing what you have heard back to the speaker(s)

> Asking questions

> Displaying appropriate non-verbal signs such as good eye contact, verbal gestures, and nodding

A word about note-taking

If you are practicing deep listening, you cannot take detailed notes. If you are trying to capture everything that is said in notes, then you immediately lose all the visual clues as eye contact is not maintained. Also, you will be concentrating on writing notes rather than on listening.

I have had to work hard to train myself to take the most minimal of notes. As a former solicitor, I had become used to taking copious notes for evidential purposes. This is not required for mediation in any event, and I always indicate to the parties that I will destroy my notes after the mediation and that they are simply for my own purposes during the process.

With some practice and experimentation, you will find what works for you, but I find it useful to divide the page of a notebook into two columns, one for each party, and jot down key words, phrases, or issues. This works for me as it enables me to spot common themes or identify points of difference very quickly.

Non-verbal communication

It is often said that the words we speak only account for a small percentage of what we communicate. Important aspects of what we communicate are tone of voice and non-verbal communication and this becomes even more important when the words spoken are at variance with body language. It is therefore vital that a mediator is alert to the non-verbal signals and takes into account this important element of what is being communicated.

I am sure that everyone can relate to situations where the words spoken by someone are totally at odds with their body language or tone of voice, for example, when someone says "yes" but their body language shows that what they really mean is very clearly "no." Examples that I have come across are where facial expressions, tone of voice, and body language (crossed arms, hunched shoulders) and lack of eye contact suggested hurt, anger, and lack of belief in what was being said, namely, that they were in disagreement to what was being proposed.

Where this is the case, it is important to establish what is going on underneath the words. If you feel that there is a variance between what one person is saying and the non-verbal communication, then the best advice is to ask for clarification. For example, pose a question such as "My observation is that whilst you have said "yes" you have not really accepted what X has said, can you clarify that for me?". Also as a mediator, you need to be aware of your own non-verbal communication and ensure that this does not indicate a lack of interest, understanding, or impartiality. The best way to do this is to deeply listen, suspend any judgment, and maintain neutrality (see the upcoming section). If you fail to do so, this will eventually leak out in your non-verbal communication, and if you feel that this might be happening, take a break.

Non-verbal communication includes the following:

> Facial expressions.

> Gestures such as hand movements, waving, and pointing.

> Tone of voice, loudness, inflection, and pitch.

> Body language and posture, intonation, and pace of speech.

> **Eye contact**: Looking, staring, and blinking, or lack of eye contact. These all display different emotions.

> **Haptics**: This is communication via touch, for example, touching someone lightly on the arm can convey affection or sympathy.

> **Proxemics**: This is personal space. Depending on context and preferences, individuals will have differing levels of comfort with the amount of personal space they have.

> **Appearance**: Choices of colors, clothing, and hairstyles communicate something about us all. We are all guilty of making judgments and assumptions based on people's appearance, and as a mediator, you need to work hard to suspend such judgments and not allow them to influence your views of a party.

Practice makes perfect – an exercise in listening skills

Here is an exercise that you can do in order to practice your listening skills:

1. Find two other people to work with; ideally others who also want to practice and improve their listening skills.

2. Each choose a topic to talk about for 3-5 minutes. Choose a subject that you have strong feelings about, for example, it could be something that you feel angry, sad, or happy about. Examples could be your proudest moments (or your children's), biggest disappointments, best holiday ever, sporting prowess, favorite film, and so on. Don't name the emotion as the listener will be listening for this.

3. Decide who the speaker is, who the listener is, and who the observer is.

4. For 3-5 minutes, the speaker tells their story and the listener listens. The observer observes using the upcoming checklist.

5. For 1-2 minutes, the listener relays back what they have heard, identifying the emotion underneath the words.

6. The speaker corrects any detail and gives feedback to the listener.

7. The observer gives feedback with reference to the checklist.

8. Swap around and repeat this task so that each party has the opportunity to listen, speak, and observe.

Listening checklist

The following checklist is useful as a guideline on what to look for to demonstrate that a person is listening deeply and effectively:

List
Appeared to be involved: Good body language, eye contact, focused on the speaker

List
Listened with empathy: Gave appropriate verbal or nonverbal responses

List
Checked understanding: Asked questions for clarification

List
Demonstrated listening: Made comments/gestures to show listening

List
Understood correctly: Articulated what the speaker was thinking and feeling

List

Could repeat accurately what the speaker said

Make a note

Comments/observations

Establish trust and rapport

Rapport is about establishing a connection with people. In the context of mediation, it is important because if you can establish rapport, the parties are far more likely to feel that they can trust you and so be more open and honest. In addition, they are more likely to feel that they have they have been understood.

What is rapport?

One definition of rapport is as follows:

> *An emotional bond or friendly relationship between people based on mutual liking, trust, and a sense that they understand and share each other's concerns.*

So, how do you establish rapport?

Rapport is established when there is some common connection and an alignment of body language and communication style. Most of us do this without thinking and we naturally adopt a different language when we are with people we know well. Next time you are with a group of close friends, look to see whether the group adopts similar postures and language.

The following are tips to follow in the context of mediation.

Mirror the other person

Mirroring is a rapport-building technique in which one person adopts the physical and verbal behaviors of another. It tends to happen automatically between people who know each other well. Where you don't know the person, you can adapt your behavior to mirror the body language and communication style of the other person. For example, this includes mirroring the person's tone of voice, rate of speech, posture (for example, leaning forward, or sitting up straight), hand gestures, and word choices.

Avoid mirroring accents or copying unusual phrases, because this will be noticed. It is important to be subtle! Mirroring only works on a subconscious level, so be careful not to overdo this as if it becomes obvious, it will become counterproductive and come across as insincere. The best advice is to be alert and observant to the other person's body language and words and match this accordingly.

For example:

Susie is a very tactile person who "wears her heart on her sleeve", is very expressive facially, uses a lot of animated gestures, and speaks with a quick pace at high volume. When mirroring, you are likely to touch the other person on the arm lightly, use emotional language that matches their pace, and use more gestures when speaking.

Jack, on the other hand, is very formal in his use of language, business-like in his manner, fast-paced, quite unexpressive, and not willing to engage in small talk. When mirroring, you are likely to stand tall, engage in a firm handshake, make direct eye contact, and get right down to business.

Show that you are listening

Demonstrate active listening skills by adopting appropriate body language, eye contact, non-verbal clues, and summarizing and questioning skills as explained earlier.

Often at the start of mediation, the parties will be quite skeptical about both you and the process itself. They may be reluctant to speak in any detail, nervous about what they can and can't say, and not look anyone in the eye. They have almost certainly tried to communicate how they feel previously but have not felt listened to. If you adopt open body language, maintain eye contact, react to what the person is communicating, and check your understanding, then they begin to appreciate that you are listening and understanding their perspective. You can sense that this is happening as their body language seems to relax and they become more and more open to sharing their feelings and engaging in dialog.

Pay attention to your appearance and first impressions

Appearance does matter! It should help you connect and help you to feel confident and competent. Think about who you are meeting and what to wear. If you turn up in a sharp suit when you are meeting people who work in a manufacturing environment, then this may create an immediate barrier to establishing rapport. First impressions are vital and can lay the foundation for good rapport.

Be confident and yourself

Your body language should demonstrate confidence; a good handshake and smile are a very good start. If you are feeling nervous, it will leak out in your body language. If necessary, try the breathing and posture exercises mentioned earlier, or think of a situation in which you are normally confident, then visualize that and how you would feel in that situation. Don't try to portray yourself as something other than who you are; it will pay dividends if you act naturally and are open and honest.

Remember that confidence is simply a state of mind; it is not based on fact. Have you ever done a presentation and felt nervous only to be told by members of your audience how confident you appeared? Well it is exactly the same in a mediation context. It is highly likely that whatever you feel, you will appear confident to the parties (who will be far more nervous than you anyway!). Also, it is ok not to know everything and to make mistakes; after all, that is how we learn. Keep in mind this quote from the American author Helen Keller: *"Optimism is the faith that leads to achievement. Nothing can be done without hope and confidence."*

Try an occasional bit of disarming honesty and humor

Small talk can be important to establish rapport and put people at ease. An example might be something about a bad start to the day or problems with your journey, for example. It reveals something about you, is something that others can relate to, and shows that you are human. Making people laugh can also be powerful and can release tension, but be careful that it is appropriate!

Maintaining a sense of calmness

Things will get fraught and emotional from time to time, and we will see in the next chapter that this is an important part of the process. As the mediator, you need to maintain a sense of calm and manage your own emotions and the process so that the emotions on display do not derail the process. It is also important to ensure that the parties do not become overly stressed to the point that their ability to communicate, listen, and think logically is impaired.

There are some fascinating studies about how one person's mood can affect others. For example, psychologists Howard Freidman and Ronald Riggio found that when a group of people are in close proximity and do not speak to each other, their mood and physiology will quickly start to align with the person in the group who is the most facially expressive. The rate of breathing and heart rates of the others in the group will start to align within a few minutes. Similarly, Caroline Bartel and Richard Saavedra found that people in meetings together shared the same mood (good or bad) within two hours.

As a mediator, if you are calm and confident, you can impact the party's moods and ensure that the parties become calmer and less stressed, which will improve their communication and also make it easier for you to manage and control the process.

You also need to manage your own emotions throughout the process. This is similar to being empathetic, but also involves you becoming aware of and connecting to your own emotions, which will improve your ability to understand both yourself and others. An important thing to remember is that we all have the ability to choose our own emotional response, which can enable you to remain composed, positive, and unflappable. This is an aspect of "emotional intelligence", and there are many books and articles on the subject. (Salovey and Mayer are leading researchers and Daniel Goleman's *Emotional Intelligence – Why it can matter more than IQ* made the subject popular.)

In the context of mediation, being aware of and recognizing your own emotions and the emotions of others will be a great help. A good way to improve your skills in this respect is to get into the habit of self-reflection, particularly following mediation or other emotional situations. Name the emotions and think about how you felt and why.

If at any point in a mediation process you do feel that you are struggling to manage your emotions or you are losing that cool, calm collectedness, then the best advice is to take a break. Have a timeout and refocus, think of something else for a while, and practice your breathing and posture exercises.

Creativity and identifying needs and interests

As we saw earlier, it is for the parties to resolve the conflict or not and for the former to come to whatever solution works for them. Since there is no limit to what can be agreed in a mediation context (other than things outside yours and the parties' control) there is an infinite range of solutions available.

In your role as a facilitator, you can assist the parties by helping to identify creative solutions. The best way to do this is to put forward a number of possible options for the parties to consider or brainstorm ideas using a flip chart. Don't worry about putting forward daft ideas; the more creative you can be in offering solutions that are "outside the box" the better, as this may generate other ideas and encourage new ways of thinking. It may also encourage the parties to look for and become focused on finding solutions.

One way that you can help the parties to identify possible solutions is to help to identify their needs and interests, as it is here that the parties are likely to find some common ground or alignment, leading to a solution that satisfies both. The needs and interests are what lie underneath the factual disputes and positions that people in conflict take up.

Needs and interests are the things that are important to us all at a basic human level, and they are often the same or very similar for both parties in a conflict situation. Needs and interests include things like the following:

- ➤ Belonging
- ➤ Security
- ➤ Personal safety
- ➤ Recognition
- ➤ Retaining control
- ➤ Saving face
- ➤ Financial wellbeing
- ➤ Health
- ➤ Privacy

You will know when you are getting close to uncovering or identifying needs and interests as this is when things start to "hot up". For example:

> ➤ When parties make statements that include things such as "I want/don't want....
> I need.... I am concerned/afraid about ....what bothers me is ....
> The problem is ....My complaint is".

> ➤ Issues arise that spark argument or are expressed with high emotion.

> ➤ A party becomes animated or withdrawn.

> ➤ The party is describing how the problem is affecting mood, routine, or health.

> ➤ There are underlying themes that connect several issues.

> ➤ There is hidden care amid blame. For example, shouting at a child who runs into the road is a desire to protect. An example I have come across in a workplace context was non-provision of information with a desire not to overload a colleague.

If you can identify the needs and interests, then there is often a way of both parties getting what they want and in a way that works.

Questioning styles and techniques

By adopting skillful questioning techniques and styles a mediator can encourage parties to do the following things:

> ➤ Challenge assumptions that they have made, in particular about the other person's intentions. This is very common in practice; we are all guilty of making assumptions about others, but we can never really know what their intention is. Examples of assumptions that I come across are that one party is deliberately trying to cause harm to the other, that one party is being manipulative, that they dislike the other person, that they do not believe in the other's capability to carry out the role, and so on. In many cases, these assumptions prove to be wrong and if not, it is still important to get the issues really out there and on the table for discussion.

> ➤ Think "outside the box" by opening up the parties to different ways of thinking about the issues, the other person's motives, or how things might be resolved. This is similar to challenging assumptions but will also include questions designed to facilitate problem solving.

> ➤ Think about how life can change in the future, for example, what life would be like if the conflict were resolved. By the time parties are involved in mediation, they are likely to have been stuck in the conflict for some time and this will impair their ability to see a way out. Understand that they can take charge of their own behavior and that they do have control over the outcome. Often parties will say that things will only change if the other party changes and that moving forward or not is all down to the other person, not them. In practice, resolution will only be sustainable if both parties accept that they have contributed in some way and also have a responsibility to change too.

➤ Focus on the future and potential solutions. Questions about what may happen if there is no agreement tends to focus the parties' minds as they will often realize that the alternatives to trying to find a resolution are far worse.

➤ Understand the other person's point of view. Often, the parties have come to their point of view on the basis of incomplete information. A good example is that they have only heard half the story with other information being filled in from their own imagination or based on what others have told them, the result being that the message has been lost in translation. This may arise, for example, when a manager has information not available to other employees due to issues of confidentiality or they have simply not thought to pass on other information when they are busy doing their day job. Questions that allow the parties to explain their positions and fill in the gaps can do a lot to clarify their position and promote better understanding.

There are many different styles of questioning but generally as a mediator, you need to ask open and probing questions designed to get people thinking. This will include questions starting with "why,"" how," "what," or "can you explain?" A good way of thinking about this is to question people in such a way that you remain continually curious. Similarly, you should try to avoid asking too many closed questions that will elicit a yes or a no answer.

There are no hard and fast rules; each situation will be different and with practice, you will develop your own questioning style. However, here are some examples of questions that may be useful.

Opening questions

These are questions designed to draw out information and to get people talking and settled. Open questions are particularly useful in the early stages of mediation as a means to encourage dialogue and clarification of the issues or parties' positions. They can also be used if you sense that a party is reticent in providing detail or is holding back. Some of these questions are as follows:

➤ Could you tell me about the concerns that brought you here today?

➤ Can you explain what has been happening?

➤ Can you provide me with some background?

➤ What is your view of the situation?

Questions to get information/understanding

These are questions designed to dig a bit deeper, to obtain further detail, explanation, or clarification. They can prompt parties to think more deeply about the issues and concerns and provide further information for clarification.

The information provided in response to these questions may in themselves provide clarification and understanding, particularly where there has been some misinformation and rumors and the parties have not been communicating directly. Some of these questions are as follows:

➤ Can you give me an example?

➤ Can you tell me more about ....?

➤ Can you explain....?

➤ Can you help me understand why ....?

➤ Can you describe what happened when.......?

➤ What do you think causes...?

➤ Why is ... happening?

Questions to get at what is underneath/really important

These are questions designed to understand and identify what is underneath the issues and the parties' positions, that is, what is really important to the person. Often this is referred to as identifying the "needs and interests" of the person, which often relate to such issues as job security, need for respect, trust, recognition, saving face, and control. These questions can dispel assumptions that parties have come to regarding the other's intentions, which may lead to them understanding that there is no ill motive where they thought there was. Some of these questions are as follows:

➤ Why are you saying that?

➤ What is important to you in this?

➤ I can see that you are clearly upset/angry about .... can you explain why this is important to you?

➤ Why? (keep asking it—you'll never get past a few times)

➤ If you could have X, what benefit would it bring to you?

➤ What do you fear might happen?

➤ What concerns you most?

➤ What effect does this situation/other person have on you?

Questions to explore alternatives/solutions

These questions are designed to encourage the parties to consider alternative explanations for the other's actions or behavior, challenge their own assumptions, and consider other options to resolve matters. Some of these questions are as follows:

> ➤ What other explanation could there be for X?
> ➤ You seem to be assuming...?
> ➤ What are the consequences of that assumption?
> ➤ What do you fear might happen?
> ➤ How do you know this?
> ➤ What alternative ways of looking at this are there?
> ➤ What is it that they don't understand about your situation?
> ➤ How could you look at this another way?
> ➤ How might X be looking at things?

Questions to test agreement

These are questions designed to ensure that the agreement reached resolves all the issues, is workable, and is fully acceptable to both parties. These questions ensure that any agreement is sustainable and that agreement has not been concluded before both parties are ready or in full agreement. In practice, one party may feel that they should agree because the other is ready to do so when they themselves are not ready. Some of these questions are as follows:

> ➤ Is there any part of this that you are uneasy with? If so, what and why?
> ➤ Can you live with this every day?
> ➤ What concerns remain?

Positive reframing

Positive reframing is a fantastic tool. Positive reframing is where the mediator restates a party's statements or points of view in more neutral or positive language but without changing the meaning. Restating helps parties to appreciate that you have listened and understood them, but when restated in more neutral terms, it can encourage them to appreciate how others may view things. It also shifts the focus from the person to the behavior concerned.

Positive reframing may also help to identify the gap that exists between the two opposing viewpoints and identify the issue that needs to be resolved. This can help to focus on what needs to be done to find a solution.

Examples of statements and positive reframing are shown in the following table:

Statements	Positive restatement
He never listens to anything I say.	It is important to you that he understands what you are saying.
She is so stupid, I have told her a million times how to do it.	It is necessary to find a way to provide the right support to embed the learning.
He is always so rude and bossy.	His manner and management style are of concern.
She is oversensitive and cannot take any kind of criticism of her work.	It is important to find a way of providing feedback that will be viewed as constructive.

Think of some negative statements. This can be anything, a moan about the kids, your partner, work colleagues, or friends who have irritated you! Then restate these statements as positively as you can. You can have fun with this exercise by being as creative as you can.

Maintaining neutrality and independence

In the context of mediation, being neutral can be summed up as:

> ➤ Not being affiliated with either side
> ➤ Maintaining the process in a way that is mutually acceptable to both sides
> ➤ Having no personal interest in the outcome
> ➤ Approaching the proceedings with an open mind
> ➤ Putting aside your own prejudices and values

Maintaining neutrality is important for a number of reasons, including building the trust, confidence, and respect of the parties and demonstrating fairness.

In practice, it can be very difficult to maintain neutrality, particularly where you may be acting as a mediator within your own organization and with people that you know or have some prior knowledge of. In these situations, it is far more difficult to put aside your own prejudices or views of people and not to have some preference in terms of the outcome. Also, demonstrating neutrality and independence can often be very much about perception.

The following hints and tips may help you to achieve neutrality and improve the chances of this being perceived to be the case:

> ➤ **Maintain your distance**: Wherever possible, do not mediate for parties that work directly for you or with whom you work closely. It is much better to ask another unconnected person to mediate and for you to mediate other disputes in different areas of the business. If this really is not viable, then explain fully to both parties the nature of your working relationships and ensure that both parties are happy with you taking on this role in the circumstances.

> **Treat both sides equally**: Pay attention to the time spent with each party. For example, if you do spend time speaking separately with each party, try not to keep another party waiting for a longer time than you spent with the other. In practice, this can sometimes be difficult as one person may feel the need to talk for longer and in detail and another will be very brief. If this does happen, then explaining why the other party needs more time may help.

> **Don't impose solutions**: If at any time you are offering solutions, put a number of options forward for discussion and consideration. If you propose only one solution, this may be seen as trying to move things in one particular direction.

> **Remain neutral**: Ensure that you are free of bias and set aside your opinions, feelings, and agendas. As explained in *Chapter 1, Conflict in the Workplace*, a good technique is to think of yourself as looking down on proceedings from a balcony.

> **Ensure equal participation**: Give equal consideration to each side by ensuring that you give each person an equal opportunity to talk about their positions and concerns fully. You will need to control the process if one person is dominating proceedings and doing all the talking. This might involve you intervening to ensure that the other party gets a full opportunity to be heard without interruption. You also need to be careful to challenge the parties equally; if you are continually questioning one and not the other, then this may appear (and will certainly appear to be) unfair and biased.

> **Suspend your judgment**: Don't assume that you know the answers and can spot the solution straightaway. It is a very easy trap to fall into but you will invariably be wrong as something will come up or be said that you were not expecting. Suspend your views and simply let the process flow.

Neutrality and independence are important principles; they protect you from becoming too involved and ensures parties are treated fairly and equally. It can be difficult at times but again these are skills that improve with practice and experience; if you are mediating regularly, you will quite quickly have heard most things!

Confidentiality

Maintaining confidentiality is an extremely important principle of mediation. The parties need to have absolute confidence that what they say throughout the process will remain entirely confidential. This will enable them to feel that the mediation is a safe environment in which they can say what they really think and feel and be completely open and honest.

If the parties are truly honest, then it is far more likely that the parties will achieve an understanding of each other and appreciate the impact of the conflict situation on each other.

As the mediator, you can assure the parties of the confidentiality of the process by:

> ➤ Explaining the confidentiality of the process before and at the commencement of mediation.

> ➤ Requiring the parties to sign an agreement confirming and committing to confidentiality (see *Chapter 3, The Mediation Process*).

> ➤ At the end of each session with an individual party, ensure you clarify which parts of what has been said can and cannot disclosed to the other party. Only disclose what you have specifically been given permission to disclose.

> ➤ At the conclusion of the process, clarify what, if anything, can be shared with others outside the process.

In practice, you often hear things that you may want to share with line managers or HR for good reason. However, unless you are given permission to do so by the parties, you cannot. I have found that it is important to clarify this with the person who has appointed you to mediate so that you manage their expectations from the start. You also need to ensure that those appointing you do not try to influence the outcome of the mediation in any way. It is important to appreciate that if you do breach confidentiality, this will impact on your ability to mediate in future disputes.

Do's and don'ts

As a summary, here is what I hope will be a useful list of do's and don'ts. Many of these are things that I have found helpful or learned along the way during my experience as a mediator.

Do's	Don'ts
Manage and control the parties	Prefer one parties' position to the other
Remain neutral and impartial	Make stereotypical assumptions about the parties
Offer a number of possible options or solutions for the parties to consider	Suggest a particular solution or encourage the parties towards a particular outcome
Listen empathetically and with your full attention	Assume that you can see the solution, as your assumption is likely to be wrong and the solution is for the parties to determine
Build rapport and trust	Don't get drawn in and take the conflict on your own shoulders

Do's	Don'ts
Positively reframe and summarize	Become sympathetic or antipathetic
Ask challenging questions of the parties in a non-judgmental way	Divulge anything to either party without the consent of the other
Retain a sense of calm and manage your emotions	Divulge anything to a third-party without the consent of both parties
Honor the confidentiality	

Summary

In this chapter, we explored the key skills that need to be mastered to effectively mediate, and looked at ways that you can practice and master these skills. A final word of advice is to simply give these skills a go: don't worry too much about precisely what and how you say things as you can always have another go. It is far better to try and learn from your experience, than not to try at all.

In the next chapter, we will look at how these skills relate to the mediation process itself.

>3

The Mediation Process

This chapter sets out the key principles of mediation and describes the various stages of the process. It looks at the purpose of each stage, considers when you might want to have joint sessions or individual meetings, and how the skills discussed in *Chapter 2, Mediator Skill Set*, are utilized during the process. Finally, there is consideration of some practical issues such as venue and room setup.

Key principles

A mediation process is *outside of any formal (that is, disciplinary or grievance) or legal process.* Ideally, mediation should be considered and commenced before these processes, but if this is not the case then the formal process can and should be halted while mediation takes place.

A very important principle of mediation is that *it is a voluntary process.* That means that mediation can only take place if both parties consent to do so. This is an important first step. By voluntarily agreeing to try to do something to resolve the situation, the parties have accepted that they have a choice (and possibly some responsibility) about whether to resolve the specific issue or not.

It is *confidential and without prejudice.* Anything that is said throughout the mediation process is confidential and cannot be used for any other purposes. For example, it cannot be used in any subsequent formal proceedings or legal proceedings.

It is *transformative and empowering, giving control to the parties.* The power to reach or not reach a solution is in the hands of the parties; it is the mediator's role to facilitate this. This also means that the process allows for creative solutions, so the possibilities are endless.

The mediator is entirely neutral and does not make any judgment, who is right and who is wrong are irrelevant for the purposes of mediation.

It gets people talking. People who are in conflict tend to take up rigid positions and avoid communication. Mediation teases out the underlying issue (of which there are always some) and focuses on each party's needs and interests, and deals with the parties' feelings and emotions.

It gets people listening and (hopefully) understanding each other's viewpoints.

Any solution is *future-focused.* There is often a need to get things aired and off-load issues and concerns, but once this is done and there is greater understanding of one another, the parties are more likely to be able to think about and focus on future solutions.

It *allows people to preserve dignity.* If mediation does end in one individual exiting the organization, then this can be done in a dignified manner, which protects the reputations of both employer and employee.

Stages of the mediation process

The skills referred to in *Chapter 2, Mediator Skill Set,* can be of real value and can be used in interactions and interventions with staff generally. We will discuss how these can be used in different scenarios in more detail in *Chapter 4, Beyond the Mediation.* However, if you are acting as a mediator in a dispute between two or more parties, then it is important to follow the process set out in this chapter. The process itself contains important elements that are designed to help the parties learn and understand each other better and resolve issues.

I recall being advised when I trained that it was important to "trust in the process. " I am not sure that I fully understood this at the time, but through experience I have come to accept and appreciate that this was entirely the right advice. You may feel as though you are repeating certain things and that the process is at times lengthy, but nevertheless it does pay dividends to stick to it. Shortcuts can be dangerous.

The key stages (which we will look at in turn) are:

- ➤ Pre-mediation discussions
- ➤ Meeting on the day
- ➤ Opening statements of the mediator
- ➤ Opening statements of the parties
- ➤ Joint sessions
- ➤ Individual sessions
- ➤ Reaching and recording any agreement

Pre-mediation discussions

Once it has been decided that the parties are open to mediation and you have been appointed as the mediator, the first part of the process is to engage in pre-mediation discussions with the individual parties.

If it is easy to do so, then it would be preferable to have these discussions face-to-face. However, if this is not feasible (in my practice it rarely is) then there is no problem in having these discussions over the phone or perhaps by an online voice application (such as Skype).

However you do this, it is obviously important to ensure that you arrange to make contact in a confidential and sensitive manner, and arrange the call so that the party can be assured of privacy.

Ahead of the discussions, it may be useful if the parties have been sent some information or guidance regarding mediation. I have put together a short *Guide to Mediation,* which I will generally ask those appointing me to pass on to the parties. This also gives them an opportunity to check me out if they wish to do so. Alternatively, I may send the guide following our initial conversation so that they have this for reference purposes. The main thing to bear in mind is that the parties will be anxious and nervous, and therefore may not take in all the information in one go.

The purpose of the pre-mediation discussion is threefold:

> **Explain the process**: This is to answer any queries that the person may have about the process, how it works, what it will be like, what they need to do, and so on. This often includes giving some assurance of the process and trying to allay their fears. Be careful not to over-sell here and seek to persuade a very reluctant party. You need to be honest; mediation is not an easy option and it will be difficult and emotional so the parties need to be prepared for that. You may also need to (or be asked to) talk about what the alternatives to mediation might be, for example, a grievance or legal claim. You cannot, of course, give any advice, but you can refer to how those processes work and how they differ from mediation.

> **Start to establish a relationship**: This is where you start to build some trust and rapport. This will come naturally to many people, but as we discussed in *Chapter 2, Mediator Skill Set*, think about the language that the other person is using and mirror the tone and words if you can.

> **Start to understand the issues**: This is where you start to obtain some information or clarification of the issues from the perspective of the party. This is probably more for the benefit of the party than of any real useful preparation for you as the mediator. It gives the party an opportunity to articulate their issues and concerns and start to think about how they will do this at the mediation itself. My practice is to generally let the individual talk with minimal questions for clarification or to demonstrate listening. I will then conclude with a summary of what I have heard with some reframing (see *Chapter 2, Mediator Skill Set*). A very useful question to ask here is what the person wants to happen or what are they hoping for in terms of an outcome; this can encourage parties to start to think about possible outcomes or solutions and look to the future.

You will find your own style and way of doing things that work naturally for you, but here is a list of the sorts of things that I would generally cover in a pre-mediation discussion:

> An explanation of the key principles, particularly explaining my neutrality, my role as a facilitator rather than a judge, and that the power is in the parties' hands to reach a solution.

> Emphasizing that the process is voluntary and that they can walk away at any time.

> Emphasizing the confidentiality of the process and an explanation that I will ask the parties to sign an agreement committing to the confidentiality (see the following section). I will provide a copy of the agreement in advance of the meeting so that they have an opportunity to read it beforehand.

> An explanation of the process and an outline of what will happen throughout the day.

> Detailing the opening statements and emphasizing that in the first stage, each party has an uninterrupted opportunity to make a statement (this is explained further shortly).

➤ Suggesting that the person think carefully about what they want to say and perhaps make some bullet point notes for the purposes of their opening statement. Clarify who will go first with the opening statements.

➤ Assuring parties that if they need a break during the day or wish to speak to me privately, then they simply need to ask.

➤ Explaining that wherever possible, the parties will all remain together but if necessary, we can have individual sessions. For example, if matters are circling, you feel that something is not being said, or if requested to do so.

➤ If an agreement is reached, then this may be recorded in a written agreement. Such an agreement would remain confidential unless there is agreement otherwise.

➤ Clarify the arrangements for the day, for example, arrival times, the venue, and that they should set aside the whole day.

➤ Invite the individual to contact me if they have any other queries or concerns in advance of the day.

The most important aspect of these discussions is to try and put the person at ease and to answer any questions that they may have openly and honestly. This is the start of you establishing rapport and trust so try and match your tone and words. There is a lot of information to pass on and not all of it will stick first time, hence the need to repeat much of this on the day as well.

The venue and room setup

The venue and room setup needs careful consideration and planning. Wherever possible, arrange for the mediation to take place in a private and confidential environment where the parties will not be seen or overheard by other colleagues. An off-site venue is always preferable unless you have the facilities to do this in-house safely and ideally in a different location. This is an additional cost but it is one that is well worth it. The parties will be nervous enough and meeting off-site will help to ensure that they are more comfortable and also more focused on the meeting. If you are in the work environment, there is a danger that minds will wander to "to-do lists", particularly if they can't resist checking e-mails during breaks.

You will also need to have two rooms set aside or at the very least, areas where you can break out and speak to the parties separately should this need arise. Bear in mind that some partition walls between rooms or offices can be very thin, so make sure you cannot be overheard when speaking confidentially to one of the parties. (This is another good reason to go off-site!)

With regard to room setup, this will depend on the environment and what facilities or office furniture you have, but bear in mind the following:

> ➤ Make the set up as informal as possible. For example, set the chairs so that the parties are at an angle and not face to face across a desk, as this could be a little intimidating. My usual preference is face the chairs towards one end of the table with me in the middle. That way, communication and eye contact can be directed through the mediator initially if this is necessary. In practice, as the session progresses, I find that the parties usually become more comfortable to communicate directly with each other and maintain direct eye contact.

> ➤ Desks or tables are not a necessity and in some cases can be a bit of a barrier. This will depend on what you have in the room, but be prepared to do a bit of re-arranging if necessary.

> ➤ As explained later, a flip chart is a really useful tool so arrange for a flip chart or bring a portable one.

> ➤ Make sure that some refreshments are available. It is a tiring and intense day, so you and the parties will need plenty of drinks and food at different points. In my case, a constant supply of coffee really helps!

> ➤ In practice, you often have to make the best of what you have got and the room setup or facilities may not be ideal. The main thing is to think about how you can arrange things in such a way that it puts the parties at ease as much as possible.

Timings and the length of mediation

A whole day should be set aside for the mediation session. Those involved should clear their diaries and wherever possible, not be under too many time constraints. This is something that I discuss in pre-mediation discussions so that this is made clear. Often this is met with some surprise and a bit of resistance, particularly when people have busy schedules. It is amazing how often people assume that a conflict that has been ongoing for some considerable time can be resolved in a couple of hours!

In practice, it is surprising how quickly a day goes by when in the midst of the process. It is very unlikely that the parties will want to go back to work after such an intense and difficult process, and if they do, they are unlikely to be productive.

One word of caution: be careful not to go on for too long and be aware of how the parties are coping. There is a temptation at the end of the day to get things finalized and to keep going at all costs. In a particular mediation I undertook, we were nearing agreement so we carried on into early evening. In hindsight (and from later feedback) it would have been better to have broken and come back at another time to conclude, as the parties were getting very tired and were feeling pushed to reach agreement and then came out of the process feeling somewhat battered.

If you do not manage to reach agreement within one day, it is a matter of judgment (and agreement of the parties) as to whether you reconvene to try and conclude. If, as in my example, you are close to agreement and both parties want to continue and try and conclude, then that is no problem and it would make sense to continue. However, if the parties are still some way from agreement, then you do need to question (and discuss with the parties) whether agreement is a realistic outcome. If not, it is best to call it a day. Don't feel that this is some sort of failure; it is in the parties' hands not yours. Also, mediation is always worth a try; it is a learning experience for those involved and on occasion, agreement or resolution may follow some time afterwards.

Meeting on the day

You need to carefully manage the arrival of parties on the day of the mediation. I always ensure that I arrive in plenty of time before the parties are scheduled to arrive. This allows you to be cool, calm, and collected and in the right frame of mind. It also gives you time to set up the room before others arrive.

It is important to schedule the arrivals of the parties. I would suggest half an hour apart. This avoids them turning up and bumping into each other in an unprepared way. It also allows you to have some time with each separately before you start to make sure the parties are ready to go and are settled. The parties can also have the opportunity to go through their opening statements and ask any questions about the process or how the day will go.

This meeting is also used to obtain the parties' signatures to the **Agreement to Mediate**, which ensures that parties sign up to and commit to the confidentiality of the process. I have provided a sample of an Agreement to Mediate in the appendix. At this stage, you should go through any questions that the parties may have regarding the agreement and, assuming they are willing to do so, ask them to sign it.

I am often asked what happens if one party breaches either the Agreement to Mediate or the confidentiality rule. While technically this is a breach of contract, the reality is that there is little that the other person can do about it. The costs and difficulty of pursuing a claim for breach of contract would be prohibitive and the breach has already occurred. I am very open with parties on this point and stress that the agreement is much more about a moral obligation to honor the confidentiality. In view of this, if you have any doubt about whether a party will honor the confidentiality, my advice would be not to proceed unless, and until, this is fully understood and accepted.

Once both parties have arrived, have signed the agreement, and are ready to proceed, the mediation commences with all parties meeting together.

Opening statements of the mediator

Once everyone is in the same room, then the process commences with you as the mediator making an opening statement. The purpose of this is to reiterate your role again, the key principles of the process, and an outline of what is going to happen.

You may feel like you are repeating yourself but this is an important step. In particular, it gives the parties an opportunity to further settle down now they are in the same room. In some situations, it may be the first time that the parties have set eyes on each other in some time and they will be anxious and nervous.

Your opening statement also ensures that you go through the key points with everyone present and listening to the same message at the same time. Finally, it establishes your position as having authority and being in control of the process.

Again you will find your own way of doing this, but here is a checklist of the things that I would generally cover in an opening statement.

All of these points are worth bearing in mind, so you may want to make a note:

> ➤ A thank you to both parties for agreeing to attend the mediation and for signing the Agreement to Mediate; acknowledging that this in itself is an important first step.

> ➤ You are not there to judge or make a decision.

> ➤ Your role is to facilitate the parties reaching a better understanding and if possible, a solution.

> ➤ You may ask challenging questions to encourage new thinking.

> ➤ If a solution is possible, then the power to do so is in the parties' hands; you may put forward options, but any decision is for the parties themselves.

> ➤ What is said and agreed will remain confidential unless the parties agree otherwise; nothing will be reported back without the agreement of all.

> ➤ Confirming again the confidentiality of the process.

> ➤ Clarifying that you may take some notes but that this is for your own purposes only and the notes will be destroyed at the end of the process.

> ➤ Clarify who is to go first with the opening statements and a reminder that while one person is speaking, the other is not to interrupt so that each has the opportunity to say what they want and to be heard.

> ➤ Clarifying the process that follows the opening statements.

> ➤ A reminder that if anyone needs a break / individual session at any time, then they should say so. Alternatively, you may suggest this at appropriate times.

> ➤ Clarify what will happen should agreement be reached.

Opening statements of the parties

There is no hard and fast rule about who goes first, but generally if there is one party who appears to be the aggrieved, I would suggest they go first. For example, if a grievance has been raised or there is a threat to do so by one party, then I would ask them to go first. I would also have an eye on the balance of power (or perceived balance of power) and where that may be an issue, I would ask the more junior or less powerful employee to go first.

Whatever your decision, it is important to make it clear to the parties at an early stage who you will ask to start with an opening statement so that they are aware of this; you certainly want to avoid this being a surprise once all parties are together. Ideally, clarify this during the pre-mediation discussions or at the individual sessions at the start of the day.

During this phase of the process, it is very important that while one person is speaking, the other party remains silent. This is sometimes referred to as "uninterrupted time."

The other person may have to fight the desire to jump in to clarify things they have heard or to raise a question and you can see that it is sometimes difficult for people to keep quiet. It is, however, a very important part of the process and if necessary, you need to control and enforce this. In my experience, this is quite rare but you do need to be ready to intervene if need be.

I believe that it is important that each party has this uninterrupted time for the following reasons:

> ➤ It allows parties (possibly for the first time) to relay the issues in whatever way they want to and to say what they think and feel without being interrupted.

> ➤ It encourages the other party to really listen; it may prevent the other party from thinking (or at least quite so much) about their response or next question rather than listening to what is being said and to suspend this while the other person is speaking.

> ➤ It may be the first time that one of the parties has heard things from the other person directly and to get any understanding of the background or how things are impacting on the other.

> ➤ It sets the tone for each party to respect and listen to the other throughout the mediation process.

When the first person has completed their opening statement, you invite the other party to make their statement with the same rules regarding "uninterrupted time."

Once both parties have completed their opening statements, my practice is to sum up what you have heard from both. This demonstrates that you have listened to what has been said and expressed. It is also a good opportunity to:

> **Draw any common threads together**: For example, while parties may be stating different causes for issues, they will often refer to similar consequences, such as a communication breakdown, stress and impact on health, or impact on the business. They may also express a desire for a common outcome such as a return to work or an improved relationship. It is helpful to identify these.

> **Identify the issues identified by both**: This is a summary of the main points referred to by both, highlighting those where there is some commonality and those where there is a different viewpoint. This can start to help to narrow the issues and agree a structure of which issues are to be explored.

> **Positively reframe the issues that have been stated**: For example, if one party has stated that they feel totally excluded, this could be reframed as "the concern is that you do not feel included."

> **Identify, if possible, the gap between them**: In the example mentioned, the gap might be how much information, consultation, and inclusion is realistic and appropriate in the circumstances, and what needs to be and can be done to ensure a feeling of inclusion.

Once you have summarized the issues, you can choose how to best proceed from that point on. If you feel it necessary, you can separate the parties and discuss the issues with them separately, obtaining their reactions to what they have heard, and identifying any areas of common ground. In practice, I would only do this if absolutely necessary. For example, I have had situations where one party has been totally shocked by what they have heard and needed some time to digest and understand it.

Wherever possible, I would suggest that you keep the parties together so that you can facilitate a discussion on the points raised with everyone present. If you do proceed in this way, it is helpful to propose some sort of structure to the discussion and agree this with the parties.

Joint sessions

Throughout the process, there can be a combination of both joint sessions and individual sessions. The former is where all parties are present in one room together. The latter is where the parties separate and the mediator then speaks to each party separately in turn. We will discuss when it might be necessary to separate the parties and have individual sessions, but in my experience it is generally preferable to keep the parties together in one room as much as possible.

It is during the joint sessions that the most progress is often made as the parties hear things directly from each other and begin to get a better understanding of how the other is feeling and perceiving things. It is not uncommon for this to be the first occasion where there has been the time and space or opportunity for the issues to be aired in this way and directly with each other. It can get emotional and fraught from time to time, but this is an important part of the process. In my early days as a mediator, I worried if things became difficult and would tend to break out into individual sessions; with experience, I now let the joint sessions flow and will only intervene or separate parties if I think that it is really necessary. Many of the mediations that I now undertake will not include any individual sessions at all.

Following the "uninterrupted time" opening statements stage, the interaction and dialog generally becomes a bit more natural with one person speaking and another replying, commenting, or questioning.

Here are some tips on how to manage the joint sessions:

> It is always helpful to suggest a structure to the discussion and agree the points or issues to be discussed. As one issue is resolved or understood sufficiently, you can move the discussion on to the next in order to maintain progress.

> You need to keep an eye on the exchanges and ensure that both parties are getting an equal opportunity to speak and be heard without constant interruptions.

> Ask each party in turn to comment on what they have heard, or give a view on a particular issue or proposal as a means of encouraging equal participation.

> If you feel that one party is not hearing what has been said, a good tip is to either positively reframe the statements or ask the "non-listening" party to restate what they have just heard.

> Keep track of any areas of agreement or common threads.

> It is handy to have a flip chart available so that you can start to put up the issues or areas of agreement on the flip chart. If individuals can visualize where they have got to, it can often help them maintain focus.

> Summarize regularly and clarify what, if any, progress has been made.

> Allow the parties reasonable freedom to discuss the issues; you will often find that other issues or, indeed, areas of agreement emerge. However, if you feel it is really going off at a tangent, then it may be helpful to restate the issues, summarize any progress, and clarify what issues are to be discussed next.

> Keep an eye on how the parties are doing. Mediation is an intense, difficult, and tiring process. While you will want to maintain progress, if you feel that the parties (or you) need a break, then suggest this. It is counterproductive to continue in such circumstances.

The main things to bear in mind when you are managing joint sessions is to ensure that you demonstrate and maintain your neutrality at all times and facilitate the discussions in such a way to maintain progress and focus. Try to resist looking surprised at anything you hear and try and challenge each party equally. You need to balance maintaining control and authority over the process as well as letting the process and dialogue flow; with experience, you will learn when and when not to intervene.

What to do if things get stuck

Parties often struggle to move forward, particularly if a conflict has been ongoing for some time. As we saw in *Chapter 1, Conflict in the Workplace*, people can get stuck in a conflict situation to the extent that it starts to define them and it can be difficult for them to see beyond the conflict. It is also not uncommon for one party to be able to move on quite quickly while the other struggles to do so.

If you feel that things are getting stuck, that progress is not being made, or that one or more of the parties are circling, there are a number of things that you can try:

> **Positively reframe the issues**: This helps to focus on the gap between the parties and where they can further explore where a solution might lie. An example might be where there are disagreements regarding performance, manageable workloads, and priorities, where a positive reframe could be "the issues concern how to maintain appropriate workloads and set realistic performance targets acceptable to both parties."

> **Summarize the position**: Identify what has been agreed so far and what remains to be agreed or discussed. This can help parties to see what they have achieved so far and refocus. If in doubt, my advice is to summarize; if nothing else, it gives you some thinking time!

> **Use a flip chart**: Writing up the issues on a flip chart can often be a useful way to help visualize the position.

> **Pick an easy issue**: If one issue is causing particular difficulty, you could suggest that you move on to discuss other issues first. It might be that as you get agreements or understanding on other issues, the difficult issue becomes less difficult or important. However, you must come back to the unresolved issue; do not leave it unresolved.

> **Move to individual sessions**: Separate the parties and speak to them individually (see the following section). You can then explore in more detail what is preventing one party from moving on and what they would need to move forward or resolve matters. Alternatively, the reason for not moving forward may be due to them holding back from sharing what they are thinking and feeling in a joint session.

> **Take a break**: Allowing some time for parties to reflect can often result in movement; it is amazing how a little bit of reflection over a lunch break can help.

> **Defer to the parties**: Ask the parties what they want to do next. It may sound a bit odd, but don't be afraid to put it back to the parties; it is in their hands to move forward or not. If things are getting really stuck, clarify whether the parties want to continue with the process.

> **Propose options**: Offer a number of options for the parties to consider. There are no hard-and-fast rules here but try to offer two or maybe three options. If only one option is put forward, this may be seen as leading the parties down a particular path. The more options you suggest, the more opportunity there is for this to spark both discussion and alternatives.

➤ **Brainstorm**: Invite the parties to brainstorm ideas about solutions and what is possible. Be clear that there is no such thing as a bad idea.

➤ **Look to the future**: Ask the parties to think about what life would be like in the future if there is no solution. This invites a bit of reality testing on what the alternatives might be.

➤ **Look to the future again**: Ask the parties to think about what life would be like in the future if there is some form of agreement. This helps parties to contemplate life in the future without conflict.

➤ **Ask the parties what is needed**: Ask the parties what would need to be done for them to move forward. There are all sorts of things that may arise here, for example, a feeling that they have not really been heard and understood, that any apology is not really genuinely meant, that nothing will change, or that they do not believe any agreement will be kept to. This may help to identify issues that need further exploration and generate further discussion. A few examples of some questions that you might ask here are:

> ➢ What would give you the reassurance that you want?
>
> ➢ What would you like to see happen in the future?
>
> ➢ What else could be done?
>
> ➢ Are there any other alternatives?
>
> ➢ What are the gray areas for you?
>
> ➢ What could be done to improve x?
>
> ➢ What can you do differently?

These questions will help you to move things forward and help to move the parties from focusing on what is wrong to what is possible and then to what is going to happen. However, be careful that you don't get into a position where you are "flogging a dead horse" and starting to impose or push for agreement where there is none. On occasion, you have to accept that the parties cannot move sufficiently to reach agreement, and it is an important principle of the process that the parties have the power to decide this themselves. As a mediator, we do what we can to assist and encourage the parties to fully explore all the possibilities, but we also need to learn when to stop.

Individual sessions

Individual sessions can be useful in certain circumstances as they allow you an opportunity to discuss issues with one party confidentially and without the other party being able to overhear what or how things are being said. This often means that the parties will open up and share things that they would not want to say in front of the other. It also allows you to dig a bit deeper with challenging questions and engage in some reality testing.

If you do have individual sessions, you will engage in "shuttle diplomacy." You will be moving between the parties and going from room to room positively reframing and reflecting things that have been said by one party to the other, putting forward proposals, or providing information to the other. It is extremely important to ensure that you pay very careful attention to confidentiality. At the end of each individual session, I always ask the person concerned to clarify what I am and what I am not permitted to share with the other party. This is vital to build trust and encourage complete honesty.

The disadvantage of individual sessions is that the parties do not engage directly with each other and some aspects of the messages inevitably get lost. Also, if one party is not willing to share information or feelings, then this can make it very difficult to restore any trust or understanding in the relationship between the parties, which may well not bode well for the future. The advantage is that it may help things get unstuck as the parties may be more willing to open up and share things they have not brought up before and (assuming you have consent), you can manage how the communications are reflected back.

As with most things, there are no hard and fast rules. With experience, you will learn to judge when it is right to have individual sessions. That said, you may want to consider proposing individual sessions in the following situations:

➤ Where one (or both) parties are struggling with the process in some way. For example, you sense that one party is becoming tired and no longer listening to what is being said.

➤ If you feel that one party is not engaging well, for example, they are struggling to articulate themselves or having difficulty digesting what has been said.

➤ Where issues appear to be circling, by which I mean that the discussion is going around and around the same issues without any progress being made.

➤ Where one party is becoming overly emotional or is behaving in a way that is having a negative impact on the other. This is a difficult one as emotion is good and ideally you want to let it run as far as possible. However, if one party is becoming angry and this is impacting on the other, then you may need to take a break.

➤ Where you sense that one party (or possibly both) is holding something back and are not being entirely open and honest. It is difficult to describe this, but you simply get a feeling that there are unsaid and unresolved issues.

➤ Where what one person is saying is at odds with their body language and tone and you feel that there is something underneath this. This could be where one party is saying that they agree or want to move on, but you do not feel that they have understood or accepted the other person's perspective and you want to check the true extent of their agreement.

If you feel that individual sessions may be most beneficial in a particular situation, then you should be confident in using them. While the perception may be that joint sessions are more useful, if a situation is not "ready" to be dealt with, individual sessions can be extremely useful.

Managing an individual session is a little different to a joint session. When dealing with one party alone, the dynamic is immediately altered, for example, the party will often relax more, become a lot more vocal and firm in the views that they are expressing, or make concessions that they do not want to make in front of others. One example that I recall in particular is where one party disclosed to me how a conflict situation was impacting on her health and causing her real concern and worry. However, she was adamant that there was no way she was going to disclose this to the other person as she felt that this would be a "win" for them.

The following are some of the things you can do when engaged in separate meetings:

➤ You are able to challenge parties more directly than you might in a joint session where you have to ensure you are challenging in a balanced way. This means that you can reflect things back to the party, ask for reactions to what they have heard, or ask them to consider alternative explanations or options in a more direct way.

➤ You can check any observations or concerns you may have regarding any inconsistencies between what the person is saying and their body language, tone of voice, or facial expressions.

➤ You can discuss the alternatives to reach an agreement, what this means to the individual, and what other realistic options there are.

➤ You can challenge the judgments that one party or another have made about the other; often this may involve challenging assumptions that have been made.

➤ You can share observations regarding the impact of behavior on the other party. For example, you may ask a question such as "can you understand why x felt undermined by what you did?"

➤ You can explore the party's intention and motivation, their contribution to the situation, and what they are prepared to do to change things. An example of a question here could be "what could you do differently that might encourage x to act in a different way?"

Exploring these issues in separate meetings is designed to promote honesty and openness and encourage parties to acknowledge that they have a responsibility to change things for the future if they truly want to resolve matters.

Reaching an agreement

As you progress through the process, it will begin to become clearer what the issues are and what is and is not agreed. *Keep a note of any agreements* as the day progresses so that you can refer back and clarify the terms or extent of any agreement at various stages.

It is always a good idea to take stock at regular intervals and summarize progress or otherwise even without progress. This helps parties to remain focused on the issues and also to realize what progress has been made; sometimes it can come as a surprise how much has actually been agreed along the way.

As you start to narrow the issues, it is often very helpful to agree what remains and to put these issues up on a flip chart. You can then structure the discussion around these issues and start to facilitate discussion around potential solutions.

Drafting an agreement

If you get to the point that an agreement is being finalized, then my practice would usually be to commit this to writing. The purpose of this is to ensure that the parties are clear on what is being agreed and that they sign up and commit to this. That said, there are some situations when a written agreement may not be necessary, for example, where the mediation has resulted in a better understanding between the parties and that is sufficient.

Involve the parties fully

It is important to finalize any agreement with the full participation of the parties. I would not recommend that you draft an agreement on their behalf and then ask them to sign it, as there is a danger that you have misinterpreted the agreement and will impose something on the parties that does not reflect their understanding. It is far better to agree the wording with the parties jointly so that they are fully involved in finalizing and concluding the agreement.

Be careful at this stage to *make sure that both parties are fully in agreement.* I have had a number of situations where the words spoken suggest agreement but the body language suggests otherwise. In other situations, there is a feeling that one party might feel a bit worn down by the process. If you sense this, I would suggest having a break and some individual sessions to check what else needs to happen for resolution or agreement. It might be tempting to ignore these signals or push for a settlement as that can be seen as success, but in reality this is likely to be short-lived if you have not really secured a full agreement that is workable or understanding.

Apologies

In practice, apologies can cause difficulties in reaching an agreement. An apology from one of the parties (or on occasion both) can be extremely powerful in helping to resolve matters. However, I have had a number of situations where an apology has been given but the other party does not believe it to be genuine. Where there has been a loss of trust, there is often a perception that it is easy for someone to apologize as an easy option but that the apology is not really meant. In these situations, examples of very useful questions are:

➤ On a scale of 1-10, how effective is the apology that has been given?

➤ What would you want it to be?

➤ What would make it a 10 (or what do you want)?

➤ What else would help?

To share or not to share

One final thing you will need to clarify is who (if anyone) the agreement can be shared with and confirm this in the agreement. It might be useful to share the agreement with a line manager or HR professional so that they can support the parties following the mediation and check in to make sure that the agreement is being implemented. However, it is for the parties to decide and agree this between them.

Reviewing agreements

It might also be useful to include a review process as part of the agreement. A provision could be made that you (or maybe someone else) reviews the progress in two or three months' time. This may also be useful support following the mediation and may be an encouragement to do what has been agreed, but again this is up to the parties.

There are some examples of agreements provided in the appendix that may help to give an idea of the sort of things that might be included. However, the agreement can cover anything the parties feel helpful or relevant. The main point is that there is no need for anything complicated or detailed; what is important is that it is clear and understood by those concerned.

Summary

In this chapter, we have looked at the key principles of mediation and how these apply to the process itself. Each stage of the process has been explored with guidance provided for the key stages, including how and where the skills that we looked at in *Chapter 2, Mediator Skill Set*, come into play. You now have skills and knowledge of the process to put all this into action and start to gain the experience necessary to develop your skills. As you practice your skills, it is important to reflect on every mediation session you undertake so that you continuously improve and gain from each experience. This is particularly necessary as, due to the nature of the process, it is not possible to get any real feedback from others. Good questions to ask yourself following any mediation are: *"what went well....what did not go so well..... what would I do differently and how can I improve"?*.

In the next chapter, we will look at how the mediation skills and elements of the full process can be used to improve your conflict resolution skills on a day-to-day basis.

> 4

Beyond the Mediation

In this chapter, we will look at what you might need to do following a mediation to ensure that any agreement is sustained and that relationships continue to work and even improve. We will also look at how the mediation skills and techniques can be used to improve your day-to-day management of employees. These skills can increase employee engagement and help you to positively manage conflicts outside of a full mediation process.

How to sustain an agreement

A one day meditation session can often achieve great things. In some cases, dependent on the issues and how far the parties are able to move or achieve understanding and reconciliation, the parties can resolve things fully during the day. If so, you go away with some confidence that the agreement will be sustained and that the parties will co-exist in a better way than before. However, in other cases the agreement reached at the end of the mediation session may only be the start of a journey and one or both of the parties will have to work hard to change the way they behave and sustain this. Also, if one or sometimes even both of the parties struggle to keep to the agreement, it may be difficult to restore trust and things may start to unravel again. There are a number of things that you (and in some cases others) can do to try to support the parties following the mediation where this is necessary:

> **Build in a review mechanism to the agreement**: This is of course entirely up the parties to decide and therefore not in your control. However, a review can be very useful as an opportunity to revisit the agreement and to take stock of what progress has and continues to be made. The review can be carried out by you or alternatively with another person such as a line manager or HR professional; again this is entirely up to the parties to decide and determine. The question of whether or not a review would be a useful option is something that you could propose for the parties to discuss, along with other options. You just need to be careful not to impose any terms or seek to influence this. In practice, I have found that most parties welcome a review as this gives them some reassurance regarding the commitment to the agreement.

> **Share the agreement with others**: Obviously you can only do this if the parties agree and consent, and if so this should be clearly expressed in the agreement. However, if this is agreed then this can also be useful as it allows the person with whom the agreement has been shared to check in with the parties to see how things are going and whether the agreement is being implemented. In the majority of cases I have been involved in, the parties have been happy for the agreement, or at least elements of the agreement, to be shared with others. Often the line manager or HR contact has had some considerable involvement and are aware of the issues in any event so the parties have no problem with some feedback being given.

Make a note

In one case I was given consent to provide feedback to a line manager so that they could consider development needs and take some responsibility to ensure that the agreement was being followed. As the mediator, it is very important that you have clear agreement and consent as to what you can and cannot share and feed back to others outside of the process. Obviously that is then the extent of what you can share; do not be drawn into sharing anything beyond this.

➤ **Development support post-mediation**: A training or development need may have been identified with one or both parties. As the mediator, you obviously need to be careful not to suggest that this is the case in any judgemental way but I have had situations where parties have understood and indicated that they feel that they need some help and support. For example, in one case a party indicated that they were struggling to understand why the other party reacted and responded in the way that they did and that they wanted help to try and understand this better. If this does arise in some way there are a number of options dependent on the needs. For example, some training on communication skills or coaching around understanding conflict responses, people styles, or emotional intelligence may be appropriate. On some occasions this can be included in the agreement or consent may be given to discuss this with a line manager or HR contact.

The main points to remember here are that the parties are in total control of what you can and cannot share and what (if any) post-mediation support is agreed. On occasions it may be frustrating as you may feel that further support would be helpful, but this is not your decision to make or to impose. The most you can do is put forward options for discussion and agreement. Finally, it might be useful to confirm to those commissioning you to mediate that futher support may well be necessary in some cases so that they are aware of this as well and you manage their expectations.

Applying your skills day after day

The skills that we looked at in *Chapter 2, Mediator Skill Set*, are key skills that will not only be useful to you in a mediation; they will also improve your people management skills and engagement with team members. We will look at each of the skills we examined in *Chapter 2, Mediator Skill Set*, and explore how these can impact on your leadership and management abilities:

➤ **Listening skills**: Learning how to really listen to your staff is important. If you listen empathetically, your understanding of the individuals in your team will be greatly enhanced. You will begin to understand what motivates them, appreciate their communication and learning styles, how they interact with others in the team, what is important to them, and what personal issues may be impacting on their work. You will also be able to spot any changes to their behaviour which may be an indication of a problem. This does take time and it is something that often gets missed by busy managers. However, it is an important part of your job and is worthy of an investment of time. Employees who feel that they are being listened to are far more likely to be engaged and motivated so the rewards are well worth it.

➤ **Building trust and rapport**: If you have a strong relationship with your staff you have a number of advantages. Employees are far more likely to be open and honest with you in the first place. It is also easier for you to have an "adult conversation" with them and for any feedback to be taken as constructive; the employee will trust that you are doing the right thing by them. Managing periods of change and delivering bad news are also easier if there are high levels of trust and motivation; retention rates and wellbeing will all be improved.

➤ **Keep calm and carry on**: If you retain a sense of calm, this will rub off on your team. I am sure we have all come across the boss who is stressed and in a constant state of panic. The result is that they simply transfer their stress to everyone else around them. It is much better to transfer your calmness.

➤ **Neutrality and independence**: As a manager you have to treat all team members equally and fairly and apply the same standards to all. You cannot afford to show any favoritism (even if you do have favourites and there are others who you struggle to get on with!). Particularly for new managers, it can be very difficult to distance yourself from people who were once your peers but this is something you need to learn to do without becoming too distant and remote; a very difficult balance. If there are issues between team members then it is vital that you give them equal consideration in exactly the same way that you would as a mediator.

➤ **Creativity and solution focused**: If you focus on solutions rather than problems, then again this is likely to rub off on others and generate a more productive culture for your team members. If something has gone wrong, playing the blame game does not help. It is far better to look for solutions and learn the lessons. If you adopt this approach then this can improve the relationship and trust between you and your team.

➤ **Questioning techniques**: If you master the questioning styles and techniques then you will also improve your ability and confidence to have difficult conversations. This is something that about 60 percent of managers admit to avoiding rather than tackling. By using open questions you will get to the real issues and reach a full understanding of the situation. To me, this is summed up by one of Stephen Covey's *7 Habits of Highly Successful People*, namely "seek first to understand, then to be understood".

The questioning techniques also enable you to get to a position where the employee understands and accepts the need to change rather than you trying to impose this; if so then it is far more likely to be effective in securing the change. Your listening skills are of course important here too.

➤ **Confidentiality**: As much as you might want to, you cannot afford to get drawn in or involved in team gossip. It will undermine your neutrality and independence and you have to lead by example, setting a standard and acting as a role model. Also, if you are trusted with confidential information then this must be honored. If the confidential information is something that you have an obligation to pass on to others then you should inform the employee and discuss how this is to be managed.

These are all key people management skills that will improve your staff relationships and increase levels of trust and engagement. This will involve an investment of time, which can be difficult in practice, but it is the most important element of a manager's job as you can only achieve your goals if you bring others along with you.

Resolving a conflict with a colleague

If you are yourself in conflict with a colleague, whether this be your boss, a peer, or a member of your team, your mediation skills can be put to good use and help you resolve this conflict directly.

Some key tips to manage conflict situations positively and resolve difficult situations and relationships are as follows:

> ➤ **Understand your own response**: How you respond will have a huge impact on whether the conflict escalates or is resolved positively. Individuals respond differently in conflict situations; sometimes we may respond by avoidance, sometimes we may be accommodating or competitive, or collaborative and compromising. Which is appropriate at any time will depend on the issues concerned and the relationship between the individuals. Each of us tends to use one of these responses more frequently than the others; that is, we have a default response mode (for further information, refer to Thomas Kilmann's *Conflict Mode*).

> ➤ **Choose your response**: Where people get stuck in these response modes and they clash, problems will arise. Managing your response is about learning to choose an appropriate response mode dependent on the situation and the other person, rather than simply resorting to your ususal default mode of response. For example, if two people are both responding competitively then this is unlikely to be constructive towards finding a resolution; a better approach might be to accommodate or compromise on some issues in order to move towards resolution. Bear in mind, too, how your tone of voice and body language can impact and pay attention to that. Finally, if necessary, manage your own stress by using the exercises we looked at in *Chapter 2, Mediator Skill Set*.

> ➤ **Attend to the other person first**: If you feel that someone has said something critical or you are in a conflict situation then the first response is often to become defensive and to seek to justify your own position. The impact of this is to simply widen the gap between your respective positions. By attending to the other person first you are better able to manage your response. Rather than attempt to justify (which may seem defensive), take a metaphorical step back, take a deep breath or two, and then validate. This means that you should ask questions to clarify and obtain further detail and information about what has been said. This does not mean that you are agreeing with the other person; you are simply seeking clarification in an assertive rather than a submissive or defensive way.

> ➤ **Explore the need behind the want**: This is exactly the same technique as used in mediation when you are trying to identify needs and interests and getting to what is really important. To do this you need to be asking all the open questions that we looked at in *Chapter 2, Mediator Skill Set*, such as "Why is that important?", "Why does that matter?", and "Why do you want that?".

➤ **Invite the other's solution**: Be careful not to jump in too soon with your own solution as this may not fully match the other's needs and interests. It is preferable to invite the other person to put forward a solution to the issue or problem. Here you would be posing lots of problem solving questions such as "How would you see us solving that?", "What would you suggest?", "What would be your solution?", and "What can we do so you get X and I get Y?".

➤ **Build a win-win solution**: By engaging in problem solving questions and inviting the other's solution, you are encouraging a collaborative approach to resolving the differences between you. To ensure that you achieve collaboration remember that there is no such thing as a bad idea. Don't dismiss any ideas (however daft you think they might be!). Recognize that the idea has some merit but then express any concerns and discuss solutions to these concerns.

➤ **Listen**: During all the mentioned stages, your deep listening skills should be in full use. Remember, you should be listening to what is underneath the words, remain aware of non-verbal clues, and identify the emotions that lie within and beyond the other's speech.

➤ **Some words are better than others**: Don't get too hung up on precisely what words to use but there are some phrases that are best avoided. In particular try to avoid using any universal terms such as "you always", "you never", "you should", or "you'll have to". These simply put pressure on the other person to justify themselves and is likely to lead to them becoming defensive. A better approach is to use such phrases as "My view is", "My perception is" or "My concerns are".

➤ **Use "I" statements**: Also, it is better to talk from your own point of view, using "I" statements such as "I think" or "I feel", rather than "You" statements, which sound more judgmental. Focus on the behavior, not the person and avoid language that might be taken as an attack on them.

➤ **Be clear**: It is far better to use clear language and to talk straight. Don't beat around the bush and talk in riddles; it is best to avoid analogies and figures of speech to avoid misunderstandings (no pun intended).

➤ **Choose a good time and place**: Think about the best time and day of the week to discuss the issues. There are no hard and fast rules here but generally I would suggest you avoid the end of the day or week and the best advice is to deal with it as soon as possible. You also want to ensure you can have the conversation in a private place without others overhearing and where you can talk face to face, with no distractions or interruptions.

➤ **Make an appointment**: This might sound a bit odd but this is also about managing your response to the conflict by respecting the other person. It also means that the other person is not caught off guard and unprepared, which can reduce the constructiveness of the conversation. A good approach is to tell the colleague that you want to discuss an issue and ask when would be a good time. If the answer is no, then either suggest another time or ask the colleague to do so. Be careful not to let it drift; it is important to deal the with rather than avoid it.

> ➤ **Take turns and don't interrupt**: In order to ensure that each of you is able to speak fully and be listened to you can use the "uninterrupted time" technique used in the opening session in a mediation process. That way you both take turns being the speaker and listener without interruption.

> ➤ **Acknowledge your contribution**: There is always something that you will have contributed to in the situation. It might be a delay in dealing with the issue or not recognizing the extent of the problem. It is always powerful to acknowledge this and accept it.

> ➤ **Don't get hung up on right and wrong**: Focusing on who is right and who is wrong is counterproductive; as we saw in *Chapter 1, Conflict in the Workplace*, this is irrelevant; it's far better to focus on the future and on solutions. In the vast majority of cases it is better to be happy than to be right.

> ➤ **Deal with obstacles**: If your colleague is unwilling to talk about the issue, ask them to explain the reasons why. If it is due to a fear that the discussion will become hostile, reassure them that this won't happen, and don't let it.

It is far better to take charge and try to resolve issues rather than hope that they will go away; they won't. If you don't and the conflict becomes worse, then it will impact you (and probably the other person too); if this happens and it starts to get to you, it is like "letting someone live rent free in your head". I am not suggesting that it is easy to manage conflicts in which you are one party and you will need some resilience; however, the alternative is far worse. In the wonderful words of Albert Einstein, "The definition of insanity is doing the same thing over and over again and expecting different results", so if one approach does not work be persistent and try something different.

Helping others resolve a conflict

Following the mediation process we explored in *Chapter 3, The Mediation Process*, is obviously one mechanism to resolve conflict, but it is not always appropriate. Here, we look at situations that may require some management intervention but not full mediation.

Situations where this may apply are where the conflict situation is not too deeply rooted and you are intervening at a relatively early stage. This is particularly the case where you as the manager have a good relationship with both employees and will be seen as neutral, and where your attempts to resolve conflicts previously have not compromised you in any way. Wherever possible, you should attempt to resolve matters between members of your team first (assuming they are unable to resolve themselves). Only if this is unsuccessful and the conflict remains unresolved or escalates should mediation be considered; it would be wrong to use mediation as a first step and as an alternative to good management intervention.

The following tips are key to resolving conflicts between employees in situations where you are not engaging in a full mediation process:

> **Intervene rather than avoid**: As stated previously, avoidance is not a good policy. It is your job as a manager to take action and once you have mastered the mediation skills you can do so with confidence. Also as mentioned, intervene sooner rather than later; do not let things fester.

> **Prepare**: Do your homework and gather the information that you need.

> **Choose a good time and place**: As mentioned, think about the time and place and make sure that you can meet where you will not be disturbed and overheard.

> **Listen**: Utilize your deep listening skills and pay attention to everything. Try to identify the emotions, needs, and interests.

> **Don't judge**: Just as in mediation, don't take sides. Remain neutral and suspend your judgement. It is important that the individuals understand that you will not take sides and that it is their responsibility to resolve the conflict proactively as adults (with support if need be).

> **Help people to see the other side of the story**: Again, as with mediation your job is to try and facilitate the employees' understanding of each other's perspectives and respective positions. You can use your reframing and questioning techniques here to help the individuals to achieve this.

> **Meet together or separately**: There are different opinions on whether you meet the employees together at all times or separately. The arguments are similar to the joint versus separate sessions in the mediation process. My view would be to meet separately first to get an idea of the issues of concern and to then bring the individuals together. To ensure that the session is constructive and the individuals have a full opportunity to speak, be heard and listen, and you can use the"uninterrupted time" technique and control the process in the same way as you would in a mediation. For example, summarize from time to time, identify the gaps and common threads, and encourage a focus on possible solutions.

> **Ask for specific actions**: Ask each person to describe specific actions they would like the other person to do to resolve the situation. By concentrating on actions the focus is on behavior rather than the character of each person. If the individuals struggle with this or you need to explore this further, a good technique is to ask each to identify what the other can do more of, less of or start doing.

> **Involve all in the solution**: Again just like mediation, the individuals should be fully involved in coming to their own solution; your role is to help facilitate this.

> **Review and monitor**: Set a time to review how things are going and monitor carefully to ensure that the commitment to resolve does not waiver.

Again, one of the key principles here is to intervene without delay rather than avoid and delay. As with mediation, it is important that you try to remain neutral and facilitate a resolution between the individuals concerned without taking sides. That said, if you become aware of inappropriate behaviour then this needs to be dealt with separately with standards of appropriate behaviour being made clear when necessary.

Case studies: mediation in action

The following are examples of the situations in which I have been asked to act as a mediator and an indication of the outcomes. Where necessary, and to ensure that confidentiality is maintained, I have changed some of the details.

Return from sick leave

This was a mediation involving a relatively newly appointed manager and a member of his team. There had been some relationship difficulties with the employee and others for some time culminating in the team member losing his temper during an argument with his manager. There then followed a period of sick leave for stress-related illness. The mediation was commissioned in order to assist with a return to work.

During the mediation session it quickly became clear that the employee had been unsupported by others in the organization for some period of time and effectively this was "taken out" on the new manager. The employee was also struggling with work demands due to changes in his role and a lack of training and development to acquire new skills. Some progress was made towards a better understanding of the respective positions and apologies were given from both sides, which were accepted.

The needs and interests of both parties became clear. For the employee, there was a need to support his family and provide for them. Protection of his health was of obvious importance in the circumstances and there was a need for recognition. For the manager it was important for him to save face and retain control.

The employee was clearly suffering in terms of his ill-health and I had some concerns about the employee's ability to make decisions regarding the terms of any agreement. There was discussion over a potential exit but this was not the outcome that the manager wanted. Due to concerns over ill-health at the time and in order to avoid an agreement being concluded in circumstances where one party was not able to think clearly, the process was suspending pending further health support. When we reconvened, an agreement was reached putting in place personal development support and clarity over reporting lines and responsibilities. The relationship remains good and trust appears to have been restored. The resolution met the needs and interests of both parties, the employee's health improved, and he remains employed and earning and is getting the development support necessary to carry out his responsibilities. The manager has clear reporting lines established; external factors were identified and apologies made.

This case study illustrates some of the following things:

> ➤ How stress can impact on an individual's ability to think clearly and logically (*Chapter 1, Conflict in the Workplace*).

> ➤ How it can be dangerous to rush towards an agreement too quickly. Had the mediation continued, an agreement could well have been reached on the day but this would not ultimately been the best outcome for either party (*Chapter 3, The Mediation Process*).

> ➤ How it is important to listen to what is underneath the words; the employee was indicating agreement but it was clear from his body language and demeanor that he was struggling with the process (*Chapter 2, Mediator Skill Set*).

> ➤ How it is important to identify the needs and interests of the parties as it is here that the solution can be explored (*Chapter 2, Mediator Skill Set*).

Return following grievance

A grievance process had been completed in respect of allegations of bullying and harassment, which had been upheld, but had not resulted in the dismissal of the perpetrator. A mediation was commissioned to try and help to manage the return to work of the employee who had made the complaint and following a period of stress-related ill-health absence.

As is often common in a situation where mediation is considered necessary, there was a fair divergence between what one party felt the position to be and the other party. There were also issues that had been bubbling away for some time and had not been addressed.

The mediation enabled the parties to air a number of historical matters that had previously not been aired and to gain a far better understanding of their positions. They were able to clarify a number of misunderstandings or incorrect assumptions that each had made. The returning employee felt that there would be a lot of bad feeling regarding the complaint having been raised against another colleague and the mediation allowed the employee to receive the reassurance that was necessary and to put in place some support mechanisms.

The mediation (and subsequent coaching support) enabled the individual who had brought the allegations to return to work and be reintegrated into the team.

This case study illustrates the following things:

> ➤ The need for parties to feel that the history has been heard and understood before they are able to move on towards resolution of conflict (*Chapter 1, Conflict in the Workplace*).

> ➤ How assumptions regarding intentions are usually (maybe always) wrong and the need to clarify or question thinking in this respect. The questions discussed in *Chapter 2, Mediator Skill Set*, can be useful here.

> ➤ That there may be a need for further support after the mediation, which was discussed earlier in this chapter.

Personality conflicts

A number of mediations have involved disputes arising as a result of personality conflicts, or conflicts due to different management/communication styles. In some cases this is between a manager and team member but in others it may involve peers. In either case, resolutions have been achieved through things such as a greater understanding of the impact of behaviors, agreements regarding communication methods (for example, face-to-face rather than e-mail, and raising issues directly with each other), setting objectives, regular one-to-one feedback, and clarity regarding roles and responsibilities. Often, there is also clarity regarding assumptions that had been made regarding the other's intentions; for example in a couple of cases there was a misplaced concern that the team member had wanted the manager's job and did not accept their appointment or authority. In others, there was a concern that one party did not fully appreciate the other's capability.

These cases illustrate the following things:

> The benefit of mediation, enabling issues to be raised and responded to in a safe environment. If, as the mediator, you are asking questions to get to the needs and interests of the parties then inevitably things come out and things are said that have not been said before, leading to a better understanding (*Chapter 2, Mediator Skill Set*).

> The benefit of mediation in allowing creative solutions to be used, which would not usually arise from other processes (*Chapter 2, Mediator Skill Set*).

> The importance of allowing the emotions to surface so that each party can directly see and hear how the situation has impacted on the other. This can be very powerful as often each party is locked in their own conflict and have failed to appreciate that the other party is also suffering, and that it is not their intention to hurt the other person. This particular point demonstrates the advantage of joint sessions as discussed in *Chapter 3, The Mediation Process*. Conversely if, as in one case, a party is supressing their emotions and refusing to let their feelings show (or at least trying not to) for fear of letting their guard down, this can prevent progress.

> The need to establish sufficient trust and rapport, to enable and encourage parties to be open and honest (*Chapter 2, Mediator Skill Set*).

Bullying and harassment

A number of cases have concerned allegations of bullying and harassment, including allegations of discrimination. Mediation can be a particularly effective way of resolving issues of this nature, as in the vast majority of cases the alleged perpetrator has no real understanding of the impact of their behaviour. I may be an eternal optimist but in my experience it is only in a very small minority of cases that individuals either mean to bully or harass or don't care what impact they have.

In one case, there was particularly shocking homophobic harassment (which one party considered to be banter); once the parties began to talk directly about the issues and the impact was understood, the dispute was resolved quite quickly and genuine apologies were given and received. In this particular case, it was a classic example of the parties concerned not having spoken directly to each other for a number of years; once they were in a room together and in an environment where it was safe to have some dialog, they were able to explain their own positions and listen and understand each other.

These cases illustrate the following:

> ➤ The importance of maintaining neutrality and independence (*Chapter 2, Mediator Skill Set*). This can be a real challenge when you hear (what to you) are shocking details of potentially discriminatory conduct and behaviour.

> ➤ The importance of appropriate questioning styles and techniques; using questions which challenge without judgement, reflecting on things, and checking understanding (*Chapter 2, Mediator Skill Set*).

Summary

In this chapter, we looked at what you (or others) may need to do beyond the mediation in order to try and help the parties to continue to work towards resolving the issues and repairing the relationship. We also looked at how the mediation skills and elements of the process can be used in other situations in order to help you resolve conflict situations that you may come across yourself or to assist colleagues to resolve. Finally, we looked at some of the scenarios that arise and examples of how mediation can work in practice.

I hope that this book has started you down the path of attaining greater skills and confidence to assist others who are in conflict, to better manage conflict situations with others, and to improve your management skills. That might be a tall order in one book but my concluding piece of advice is to go and put the skills into practice. Generally it is far better to try and to fail (and to learn from that), than to never have tried at all. Remember that while words can hurt they can also help to heal. If you don't try then there is no opportunity to heal the hurt and I cannot describe adequately how rewarding it is when you have played a part in doing so.

Agreement to Mediate

Included here is an example of what is called an Agreement to Mediate. This is used to formalize the mediation process, and is absolutely essential as it allows you, as the mediator, to take control of a potentially difficult situation. Use this as a template when you are required to conduct a mediation. Hopefully, it should also give you an insight into the role of a mediator and a further insight into how the process works.

A ....

B......................................

(Collectively the "parties") hereby agree to mediate their dispute on the following terms and conditions:

1. **MEDIATION PROCEDURES**

   1.1 The mediation shall be held and conducted according to this Agreement to Mediate ("Mediation Agreement").

   1.2 The mediation is "Without Prejudice" and any settlement reached in the mediation will not be binding until it has been reduced to writing and signed by each of the parties.

   1.3 The mediator cannot be subpoenaed to give evidence.

2. **MEDIATOR**

   2.1 The parties agree that [   ] of [   ] will be the "mediator".

   2.2 The parties and the mediator recognize that the mediator is both impartial and neutral.

   2.3 The parties recognize that the mediator does not offer legal advice or act as a legal advisor for any of the parties.

3. **PLACE AND TIME OF THE MEDIATION**

   3.1 The mediation will take place at [   ]starting at [   ]

4. MEDIATION FEES, EXPENSES, AND COSTS

4.1 The mediator's fees and any other expenses associated with the mediation will be met by the organization.

5. PRIVATE SESSIONS

5.1 Information gained by the mediator through such a session and any other sessions or communications as part of the meditation process is confidential unless (a) it is in any event publicly available or (b) the mediator is specifically authorized by that party to disclose it.

6. CONFIDENTIALITY

6.1 The mediator and the parties undertake to one another that they will maintain confidentiality in respect of all statements and matters arising throughout the mediation process.

7. TERMINATION OF THE MEDIATION

7.1 Any of the parties or the mediator shall be entitled, in their absolute discretion, to terminate the mediation at any time without giving a reason.

8. HUMAN RIGHTS

8.1 The referral of this dispute to mediation does not affect the rights that may exist under Article 6 of the European Convention on Human Rights.

9. SIGNATURE OF THIS MEDIATION AGREEMENT

9.1 This Mediation Agreement is to be signed by each party.

A.

Signed:

Name:

_____

B.

Signed:

Name:

_____

C.

Signed:

Name:

_____

Lightning Source UK Ltd.
Milton Keynes UK
UKOW06f2147220215

246688UK00001B/5/P

9 781783 000661